early praise for *Your Feminine Heart*

"If we are to experience peace on this planet, we must have peace in the home. In this book you will learn how your Feminine Heart can play a vital role to make that a reality."

— AZIM JAMAL,
author of *The Corporate Sufi*
and Amazon #1 best-selling co-author of *The Power of Giving*

"This is a journey to your own Feminine Heart, a place of great depth, wisdom and power. Jenica Ashlie shows how to explore and embrace the whole of your feminine essence, and find a richer, more profound meaning in the life you lead."

— FAWN GERMER,
best-selling author of *Mustang Sallies* and *Hard Won Wisdom*

"Disillusioned and disconnected! — These are all-too-familiar symptoms for many women today. Jenica's timely wisdom is a blueprint for all women who yearn for more joy, meaning, and love in the new era of love."

— FRAN HEWITT,
best-selling author of *The Power of Focus for Women*

"*Your Feminine Heart* has come at a critical time for women — and men. This book is a gift that opens hearts and changes lives."

— SHARON KITZHABER,
former First Lady of Oregon and founder of STARS
(*Students Today Aren't Ready for Sex*)

"Jenica's new book is a gift of real insight, inspiration and down-to-earth advice helping women realize what moves their souls. Her wisdom, care and love shine through these pages and offer the secrets of feminine fulfillment. Savor, inhale and devour it completely and see what magic waits for you!"

— SATYEN RAJA,
President, *WarriorSage.com*

"In our hyper-paced, goal oriented society, intimacy is an unknown. Because millions of people do not know how to achieve intimacy, they live in lackluster relationships with themselves and others. *Your Feminine Heart* will help break that unhappy self perpetuating cycle."

— Dr. Trina E. Read,
Sexologist, Syndicated Columnist

"Jenica's book is a gift to all women seeking a deeper intimacy with their own potential for true love, but I would wish it to be required reading for all the men in my life. The Feminine Heart needs to be activated in all of us."

— Reverend Carol Carnes,
Leadership Council Member for the Association of Global New Thought

"Like lighting a few lamps, and those lamps in turn lighting more lamps, to spread the light of love and chase the darkness away; *Your Feminine Heart* shares a message to make that happen. Jenica Ashlie is all about love. This book shows you how to light your lamp (heart) and share it with the world … and what a world it could be."

— Dr. Warren Harbeck,
Columnist, *Cochrane Eagle*

"The Feminine Heart inspires and brings further strength to our souls and the truth that we must have the courage and determination to be mindful, authentic and open in all areas of our lives. This book is a must-read for those who wonder if the price for success may be too high!"

— Ann Coombs,
Thought Leader and author of the national best seller
The Living Workplace: Soul, Spirit and Success in the 21st Century

Your *Feminine Heart*

A New Era of Love

JENICA ASHLIE

Heartfelt Press

Heartfelt Press Inc.

PO Box 86011, 2106 – 33rd Avenue SW

Calgary, Alberta T2T 6B7, Canada

Toll free in North America:

1 (866) 403 • LOVE (5683)

www.yourfeminineheart.com

Heartfelt Press Inc. is a wholly owned division of *Heart to Heart Communications Inc.*

Library and Archives Canada Cataloguing in Publication

Jenica Ashlie, 1956 –
Your feminine heart: a new era of love / Jenica Ashlie

Includes bibliographical references
ISBN – 10: 0 – 9739619 – 0 – 2
ISBN – 13: 978 – 0 – 9739619 – 0 – 4

[a CIP record has been applied for]

Technical Credits:
Cover Design: JEREMY A.S. DROUGHT and JENICA ASHLIE
Interior Design and Production Management: JEREMY A.S. DROUGHT,
    Last Impression Publishing Service, Calgary, Alberta / lastimpression@shaw.ca
Editing: ROD CHAPMAN, Kimberly, British Columbia / info@navigating.info
Proofreading: SANDY GOUGH, Calgary, Alberta / sjgough@telusplanet.net
Cover Photo: *Author at Waskesiu, Saskatchewan, 1976* by BLAINE ANDRUSEK, Calgary,
    Alberta / Blaine@blaineandrusek.com
Author Photo: ANGELA CHARD, *Crystal Image Photography*, Calgary, Alberta /
    cr_image@telus.net
Pre-publication edition printed and bound in Canada by *Blitzprint*, Calgary, Alberta

Dedication

THIS BOOK IS DEDICATED TO EVERYONE WHO HAS EVER LOVED, nurtured and healed another living creature — know that through your love, you are also healing our planet.

It is with gratitude and humility that I share this message with you. Together we can create a bright new future for ourselves, our loved ones and, ultimately, this rapidly changing earth.

Acknowledgments

IN ANY ENDEAVOR REQUIRING PERSISTENCE, sacrifice and dedication, one cannot rely solely on oneself. I know, for I have tried and failed miserably.

The sacrifices that I've made in completing this book have been inflicted mostly on my family members and friends. The occasions when I wish I could have spent time with you, and played with you, were many. Often it was important for me to be alone with my Creator, asking for guidance in choosing the messages I needed to share. This took time away from you — time that will never be replaced. It is my hope and prayer that the messages contained in the following pages will make a difference for many people, and somehow make up for the time not spent with you. Thank you for your understanding and support.

A heartfelt thank you to my parents, Ann and Henry Monsebroten, for supporting my life's journey; one that you didn't always understand. A big thank you to all my dear girlfriends for your faith in both me and my message, and to the many people who have supported my work. A special thanks to my mother and to Parker's father for being there for Parker, to Ralph Eeson for his patience and support, to Braveheart for getting me to the computer at ungodly hours, to Blaine Andrusek and Angela Chard for their magic behind the camera, and to Leo Peters for reminding me of the importance of my message and for giving me hope and encouragement when I needed it the most.

Many thanks to Rod Chapman for his masterful editing and perceptive understanding of the Feminine Heart. Big hugs and deep gratitude to Jeremy Drought for his support and professional advice over the last two years. His creative insights and abilities permeate throughout this book. With deep appreciation to Sandy Gough for your excellent proofreading. God gave you eyes to see what others do not. Thank you all for meeting unrealistic timelines and demands.

My teachers have been many. I've been privileged to work closely with men and women who are making big contributions to our ailing mother — this home we call earth. I am indebted to my dear grandmother, Annie Oranchuk, and to friends Eva Pease, Gerard Grant, Cam Sinkiewicz, and Jean Gebb. Although you are not with me on this earth, your spirits were so encouraging and supportive. I felt your gentle nudging and heard your cheers every time I wrote with my open heart.

A special acknowledgement to Dr. David Chu, who helped me regain my health after a lengthy illness while writing this book. Thank you for your continued support in the maintenance of one of life's greatest blessings — vibrant health and vitality. Your understanding of the dynamics of feminine energy is reflected throughout this book. Thank you for your generous support, wisdom and guidance.

Most of all, I want to thank my son Parker, who stuck it out all these years with patience and who understood that "Mom needs to finish her book." I love you more than you will ever know. Thank you for everything you've taught me about love and relationships. This book belongs to you as much as it does to me, because without you, I would never have understood how much love the Feminine Heart can hold.

Most graciously, I give thanks to our Creator, the infinite intelligence of all life, who guides and supports me in the delivery of this message.

With love and light,

Jenica Ashlie, BA, LW
Waskesiu, Saskatchewan
October, 2005

Table of Contents

Why I Wrote this Book

If there is a book that you really want to read that
hasn't been written yet, then you must write it.
— Toni Morrison —

I N THE YEAR 2000 I DEVELOPED AND DELIVERED A WORKSHOP called "The Divine Dance" with a wonderful man named Satyen Raja. The intent of our workshop was to allow men and women to fully embrace their innate sexual expression, and to offer that to others as a gift. Based on the leading-edge work of author and teacher David Deida, Satyen worked with the men in the group and I worked with the women. Throughout the weekend the participants came together and practiced relating to the opposite sex, expressing their deepest gifts as men and women and giving each other feedback about how they showed up to others.

It became obvious that many women had a difficult time expressing their natural feminine essence. This difficulty resulted in a deep sadness and despair, leading to emotional and even physical challenges. Often, the more accomplished a woman was in her outer world, the more difficult it was for her to access and express her inner feminine spirit.

Later that year I read an article in *O–The Oprah Magazine* (October, 2000) about the results of summits that Oprah Winfrey had held in four large American cities. After speaking to thousands of women about pertinent issues facing them today, Oprah had conducted a survey asking participants to rate various aspects of their lives. In one of the questions, the women were asked to rate themselves on a happiness scale of 1 to 10. Sixty per cent of respondents rated themselves only 6 out of 10 — and these were women who had the time and means to attend an Oprah summit!

"What about the millions of women who are not so fortunate?" I wondered.

These statistics mirrored what I was seeing in our workshops. I realized that although women today have more choices, more freedoms and more possessions than at any other time in history, they are no happier for it. Because of what I saw happening around me, I knew that I could make a contribution — not only to women, but also to their families and loved ones — by helping women learn how to stop over-using their masculine qualities at the expense of their innate feminine expression.

It is time for the Feminine Heart to come out of the closet. She can no longer hide out. Whether her whispers or roars are heard by women or men, they are becoming louder. The world requires the gifts that she brings to create change on the planet. And change we must, and quickly. If we are to take a stand for the possibility of peace, and for the future of our children, timing is of the essence.

At the same time, reoccurring thoughts and insights about what is happening on our planet began to plague me — breakdown of the family structure, the angst of our young people, violence and terrorism, almost one quarter of the world's seven billion people starving and living on less than one dollar a day.

What would our world look like, I wondered, if it was filled to overflowing with the Feminine Heart? Looking at the timeless concerns of women, I began to imagine a world filled with love and respect between the sexes, safe homes, schools and streets; a world overflowing with food, housing and love; a world of healthy people in nurturing relationships; of clean rivers, thriving forests and fresh air; of peaceful communities and countries. I imagined a way of life that valued health, happiness and well-being over dominance, competition, violence and fear. I envisioned societies emerging based on the archetypal feminine qualities of nurturing, mothering, generosity of spirit, and the gifts of life freely shared.

Each woman can make a difference within her own sphere of influence, I thought. By joining others who share the same vision we can create momentum, and momentum can turn into a groundswell of women working together to serve the needs of the world's most vulnerable.

I knew I had to do something to make a difference. I decided to write a book to spread this message to as many women as I could. It was a daunting task, and many times I was challenged by the immensity of the task. I tried to not write this book many, many times, using every mode of procrastination available to woman. But Spirit would not cooperate. When I went inside and asked for guidance from my Higher Self, this is the answer I always received:

"Goddess of the light, Goddess of the light, Goddess of the light, unite!"

My workshops and speaking engagements allowed me to share my message in sporadic spurts, but I knew that a message written expressly for Feminine Hearts was needed. I visited bookstores and hunted online, but was amazed that I could find nothing that shared information about the innate gifts of the Feminine Heart.

To create a new world order — a new era of love — there must be a foundation of understanding that there is a higher intelligence, or creative life energy, that is the source of all existence. As we have evolved as a culture, we have used many words to describe this power: God, Goddess, Spirit, Love, Creator, Source, Higher Self, Infinite Intelligence, and so on. We use these terms to express an experience knowing that the rational mind cannot fathom it, that it must be embraced by the heart, not the mind. We have all had contact with this energy and, in our own way, we find labels that best express our personal connection with it.

We are all part of the whole. Masculine and Feminine Heart, God and Goddess. I have used several terms to express the oneness of all life. The beginning of each chapter starts with a "Love Letter to Myself." These letters are silent affirmations speaking to that divine aspect of myself that I call the Goddess. When I use these terms, I am referring to that all-knowing creative intelligence that exists within each and every one of us, and in all life. While you are reading this book, please feel free to use your own terms, terms that resonate deep within your own heart.

With Spirit as my guide, it is my humble intention that within these pages you will remember who you are in the depth of your radiant Feminine Heart, healing yourself and thus helping to heal the world.

Before you start, take a moment right now to make a declaration about your intention in reading this book. Why are you reading it? What do you hope to get from it? What are you seeking at this particular point in your journey? Go inside and ask for guidance, if that feels right.

Each chapter starts with a love letter that captures the essence of the message within. At the end of each chapter, you will find a section titled Musings and

Blessings. This section asks you to look at your own life and answer some questions that may bring up new ideas or old reminders.

You may choose to start at the beginning and read through to the end. When you get there, I suggest going back to review any chapters where you had difficulty answering the questions in the *Musings & Blessings* sections. Breathe deeply into your heart when you ask yourself the questions. In your answers, you will receive the gift of your authenticity — the real you.

The book is divided into three parts. Part One deals with how women have evolved. As a result of this change in consciousness, we are no longer satisfied with the status quo and crave a deeper intimacy with life. We are poised to take the helm and to lead the planet back to a place where peace is possible. We will do this by expressing more of the infinite love that is our natural birthright.

Part Two lists 28 different gifts from the Feminine Heart; one for every day of your cycle. You may want to review a new gift each day as you go through your menstrual, or moon, cycle. Each gift is unique and they are all equally valuable. Each gift that you share with another is also a gift that you give back to yourself.

Part Three shows how to leave a legacy of love while you are still on this earth. This will have far-reaching effects for others after you have passed on. In Part Three you will discover how to share your gifts to stay healthy, happy and radiantly in love with life. You will be empowered to unite with others in sharing your gifts; a force so powerful that together we will create a new era of love.

Enjoy the journey — however you discover it.

Introduction

M
Y STORY IS YOUR STORY. Many of my life experiences have been part of yours. I have survived failed relationships and divorce. I have experienced financial losses and recovered. I have suffered betrayal and a broken heart and yet again risked love. I have lost my health and regained it. I have grieved over the loss of my unborn child, and grieved for the suffering of all children. I have faced my own death, which helped me to start living. I have lost faith in Spirit, and then in times of utter darkness I have felt the hand of our Creator holding mine.

And so have you. I have met you along my path, and you have shared your stories of joy and pain with me. Although our destinies have taken us down different paths, our journey in this life is the same — to become more of who we are, and to express that essence to the best of our abilities.

Having worked as a healer, professional matchmaker, workshop facilitator and management consultant for one of the world's largest accounting firms, I have taught and counseled people on a variety of issues over the past 30 years.

My gypsy soul takes me around the globe. I've met and talked to people from the richest places on the planet, and I have lived with people from impoverished countries. What I found is that no matter what our life condition — rich or poor, stay-at-home mother or successful businesswoman — at our core we share the same yearning. We long to be seen for who we truly are — children of our Creator.

… you have a deep inner knowing that what you desire most is to give and receive love.

If this book has come into your hands, there is a distinct possibility that you know yourself to be a spiritual being whose purpose is to bring more light and love to this planet. Whether you are in the boardroom with your colleagues, the bedroom with your lover, or the bathroom with your child, you have a deep inner knowing that what you desire most is to give and receive love. That is the essence of the Feminine Heart. That is what our world needs now.

No matter how you fill your days, if you do not honor your deepest desires there will always be a sense of dissatisfaction — even if you are busy having fun with friends or working hard to make a living. Without expressing our desire to give and receive love, life will continue to shroud our radiant and beautiful light that the world so desperately needs to heal its ailing wounds.

So you go, girl: be brave. Allow your radiant light to shine so brightly that you transform your own life by finally experiencing your destiny, and at the same time helping transform the destiny of our dear Mother Earth.

Musings & Blessings

To SHARE OUR LOVE WITH OTHERS, we must start with the love that resides within. Many of us have forgotten how to access that love. We must learn to fall in love with ourselves once again, with the beauty and feminine radiance that we have to grace the world. We must become aware of the beauty, wisdom and grace that we have to offer.

With your heart open, without fear, how can you offer the best of who you are? With whom can you share your gifts of helping to nurture and heal?

The time to start sharing more of yourself is now, otherwise you are depriving yourself, and others, of the loving energy that our planet so desperately needs.

Love Letters to Myself

TRUE LOVE IS A LOVE AFFAIR WITH LIFE. Using the almost-forgotten medium of the love letter, at the beginning of each chapter I speak to the universal longing that the Feminine Heart shares. These love letters attempt to express the almost inaudible prayers we have for ourselves. Within each prayer I speak to the Goddess, that divine aspect of ourselves. Our desires, our hopes and our dreams — as well as our challenges — show up in these love letters. They come from our deepest yearning — our longing to give and receive love.

It has been said that love letters are a window into the soul. The words, tone and terms of endearment give readers a glimpse into the hopes and dreams of the writer. We share these tender words only with our beloved, and only in private. Our message is sealed with the sweet kiss of love, and it is sent with a silent prayer to the fortunate recipient.

Sometimes, when our deepest thoughts communicate our yearning and longings, we send messages to ourselves. These are love letters waiting to be received. It matters not if our silent message is one of gratitude or grief; our internal postal service ensures that our message is sent. Registered first in the mind, it is received in the limitless capacity of our hearts.

We are constantly sending love letters to ourselves. Mostly, these letters contain sweet thoughts of endearment and kind words of hope that help to heal our bruised hearts. Other times, they arrive as Dear Jane letters, leaving us with sad sentiments of lost love, shipwrecked dreams or unmet expectations. When this happens, the temptation to shut down our hearts and retreat from our divine feminine nature becomes overwhelming.

As we grow in awareness and love, we become more conscious of the messages that we send to our higher selves — to the place where we are one with our Creator. Make your message sweet. Even when we are suffering and our hearts are breaking, we can write that Dear Jane letter with the tenderness and respect that we know is our birthright, as a child of the Infinite.

Today, love letters are almost a forgotten art. When was the last time you received a heartfelt letter in which the sender exposed his innermost love and desire for your well-being? It is truly something to be treasured, to be kept in a special place and read again and again when you need to be reminded of how much you are cherished by your beloved.

Our Creator sends us love letters all the time, by answering our prayers. Yet we slough them off as a stroke of luck, or synchronicity. Synchronicity is God's way of sending you a message. Think of it as receiving a love letter from your beloved. When you receive that message, handle it with care, give thanks, and know that you are loved.

Musings & Blessings

HAVE YOU EVER TAKEN THE TIME TO WRITE A LETTER filled with endearments to your own Feminine Heart? Who knows you and loves you more than the loving and forgiving Goddess that resides within?

So often we forget to acknowledge and honor that most special aspect of our own nature, the part of us that craves to be seen in all its beauty and glory. Take a quiet time (nobody is going to give it to you) and with your favorite pen and fine paper write a love letter to yourself. Be brave and strong, allowing your most tender thoughts to be expressed. This is for your eyes only. The message is between you and your beloved inner Goddess — that divine aspect of yourself that you know to be true.

When your love letter is complete, seal it with a kiss and put it away in a safe place where you can access it any time you need a reminder of who you really are. You will love yourself for it.

The ultimate of being successful is giving yourself
the luxury of time to do what you want to do.
— LEONTYNE PRICE —

Part One

Deep Intimacy

Satisfying Our Yearning for Infinite Love

My Darling Feminine Heart:

Please open my mind and my heart
to accept the fullness of my deepest yearnings.
I crave to be filled with the love of that
divine aspect of myself that is one with God and Goddess.
In my quiet moments I know that I am blessed.
Let not my fears and pain harden my heart to the love that is my birthright
So that I may share my radiance and beauty with others,
blessing and healing others with the light of my love.
With each breath that I take in
I surrender to your love,
filling every pore of my being.
So that as I exhale, the sweet perfume of your blessings
wafts behind me as I journey throughout my days
sharing my love with others.
With love and deep gratitude I give thanks.

You can give without loving, but you cannot love without giving.
— AMY CARMICHAEL —

WORKING AS A PROFESSIONAL MATCHMAKER, the most common request I had from single women was to experience deeper intimacy in their next relationship. I knew what they wanted. Yes, a good man could help lead them to a deeper intimacy, and these women hoped to get that experience with their next partner. But I knew that they would always be dissatisfied. It was only when they had opened their hearts to the love of that deeper aspect of themselves — their feminine Spirit — that an intimate partner would make any difference.

In Part One, I will show you how to create that experience of deep intimacy for yourself. This is a necessary endeavor if you sincerely want to have deep intimacy with another.

Our Hunger for Deep Intimacy & Connection

My Darling Feminine Heart:

Oh, how I ache to be filled up
with the breadth and depth of life.
More than my body craves to feel that creative life force.
My heart and soul have longings too!
When the day is over and night shadows fall
Let me rest feeling that somehow
I have been used up
in the service of love.
Thank you, Goddess, for the experience
of intimacy with all of life.

Make each moment an occasion to live deeply, happily, in peace.
— THICH NHAT HANH —

AT SOME POINT IN OUR LIVES WE REALIZE that some kind of creative energy permeates all of life. Once we taste that sweet nectar of being connected with that creative life force, we hunger to taste it again and again. We crave to be filled by the juice of the creative Spirit.

This realization can come at any stage in a person's life. Both men and women have experiences showing that something bigger is affecting their lives. It is something that we cannot control, but can only feel and taste. This craving for a deep connection is not satisfied in the traditional sense, such as when we paint a picture or write a poem or story. It goes beyond that. This is a yearning to have a deep, intimate connection with the creative source of life itself — to become one with the world.

Assorted life experiences can give us our first taste of intimate connection with Spirit. Most of these experiences are not uncommon, especially in our early years. Suddenly, something impacts our lives and upsets our normal patterns. We are then required to adjust to a new kind of existence. This experience may come through the birth of a child, losing a dear friend, an unexpected illness, walking in nature, listening to beautiful music or falling in love. Anything that breaks through the barrier of our daily routine may stir latent yearnings within our Feminine Hearts.

Musings & Blessings

DO YOU TAKE TIME EVERY DAY TO SAY HELLO TO YOUR BELOVED? Do you give thanks for all the love residing inside that is yours to share? How do you share your love? Do you give it all, or do you throw only bits to those who you feel are most deserving at this time? In your experience, is love limited or unlimited?

Now breathe in deeply. Upon exhaling, feel your heart. Are you *being* love?

Relationships take time to grow; they require nurturing. No relationship is more important than the divine connection you have with your beloved. Other relationships will reflect the quality of the most important connection you have — your connection with Spirit.

Remember that part of you is eternal ... always has been, and always will be.

Three things are absolute and cannot be destroyed:
awareness, being, and love.
— DEEPAK CHOPRA —

The Longing for Our Natural Birthright

My Darling Feminine Heart:

The days are pale and grey when my heart aches
to be filled with the light of my beloved.
The longing is unbearable as I look everywhere to find
what I know is mine.
Then something happens and I remember
that I need not travel far.
Closing my eyes and opening my heart
I find you there, waiting for me.
I give thanks for your undying patience.
It seems I have kept you waiting for so long,
But you had never left.
 I go inside to say hello,
And once again the brilliant rays of your love
light up my life.
With deep gratitude I give thanks to the Goddess within.

> *The Lord God made a woman from the rib he had taken out of the man,*
> *and he brought her to the man.*
> *— GENESIS 2:22 —*

ACCORDING TO BIBLICAL PRINCIPLES, woman was not created out of the dust of the earth like man, and therefore she should not be treated as dirt. Earthly woman didn't fly down from heaven, so she should not be above a man's head. Woman was taken from man's ribs, therefore, according to the Christian tradition, her rightful place is at a man's side. Whatever your personal religious or spiritual beliefs, many women intuitively know this.

In the early days, for the most part, a woman was a full-time homemaker. She had time to look after the children, to create beauty in the home, to foster a family environment and to nurture her relationship with her partner. She enjoyed the communication and support she gave and received from other women. Men were happy to be the providers and breadwinners.

Of course, now the world has changed. Women are expected to carry the load. We put our time in the competitive, hard-driving, male-oriented workplace, which depletes our energy. The pace doesn't stop when we come home, either. Tasks that nurture a woman's soul are not done with pleasure or enjoyment. We are either too tired, or we do these things with a sense of urgency.

Within the last century, there have been dramatic changes. Looking back over the last two decades, life has sped up to an almost-dizzying pace. The speed at which we are moving doesn't appear to be slowing down any time soon. The promise that technology and mechanization would make life easier has proved to be misleading. We do not have more time. Technology has only increased the frenetic pace at which we are communicating and doing things. It has left us tired and unfulfilled. The toll on our emotional, physical and spiritual well-being is apparent.

Our relationships with our men and our children are suffering. Knowing that just causes us more suffering. Our health and well-being are affected by the stresses that bombard us, day after day, until we find it difficult to access the joy that we know is our birthright.

Add to that the fear and insecurity that has escalated since 9/11. We turn on the television and come face to face with the effects of our changing climate, and the natural disasters that our generation has created by polluting the world around us.

The poisons and pollutants emitted from factories and ploughed into fields in developing countries are swept up in the winds and carried over our vast oceans by toxic clouds. Then, days later, these poisons fall as toxic rain on areas of pristine natural beauty still untouched by human hands.

Germs and viruses that start in countries on one side of the planet travel to the other side, carried by passengers boarding planes destined for the far corners of our shrinking world.

I do not mention these things to alarm, but rather to remind you that our planet has become smaller, and that physically we are connected to each other, no matter where we live.

Some people are still completely asleep, or in deep denial, but most of us have evolved enough to see that our planet has become one living, breathing entity. We are no longer separate, protecting our own little territory without concern for the rest of the world. It is obvious the world doesn't work that way. We can no longer pretend that our thoughts and actions in one part of the world do not affect the rest of the world.

Not so very long ago, however, our planetary consciousness was shifting to the realization that the world was not flat. Now we have evolved to another realization — that we are not separate. The world, and the people who inhabit it, are one.

Not only are we one in a physical sense, but we are also one in our spiritual capacity. We always have been. The Spirit who resides *The world, and the people who inhabit it, are one.* in us also resides in our next-door neighbor. That same Spirit resides in people in countries around the world. We live at a time when many of us have awakened to this fact. Now we are spurred, out of necessity, to make big changes or to suffer in ignorance and despair.

Women, as part of our natural biological heritage, are acutely aware of this task. As the nurturers and caretakers of the planet, we know that we have contributed to its demise. We also know that we have the power and wisdom to make changes. We may have forgotten exactly how to access that power, but intuitively we know that it lies dormant within. We know that with the help of other like-minded people it is not too late to once again access our power. We can change the fate of our dear Mother Earth, but first we must go inside and change our internal world to reflect what we want to see in the outer world. Accessing that place within ourselves not only guides and feeds our daily lives, but when expressed, it can help to serve others.

However you have come to know the pure and clear voice of the divine intelligence within, know it is always with you. When your Feminine Heart is open, you can more clearly hear the messages that infinite intelligence is sending you.

The Feminine Heart exists within everyone. Women, men and children around the world are learning to express what lies deepest in their hearts —

love. When we are connected to that love, the pulse of life, we experience the wisdom and the grace of the Feminine Heart.

Musings & Blessings

EVERY SO OFTEN WE GET GLIMPSES AND REMINDERS of our power and our truth. When does your innate wisdom show up to remind you of your truth? Do your dreams hold special messages for you? Do you get messages that you feel in your heart when you least expect it? Utilize those times, reveling in the knowledge that is yours.

This wisdom and knowledge is the same truth that women have had access to throughout the ages. Acknowledge that, and be grateful that you now have the awareness and courage to take it to the next level, for the benefit of all.

Courage is not the absence of fear, but rather judgment
that something else is more important than fear.
— AMBROSE REDMON —

Ancient Feminine Wisdom

My Darling Feminine Heart:

Don't ask me how I know.
I just know.
The wind talks to me and shares secrets of joys and sorrows
that the rain's tears wash away.
I know there are many things that I have yet to see,
but when they come to pass I will know what to do.
Just as my mother's mother knew what to do,
and nobody told her.
She just knew.
I give thanks, dear Goddess, for that gift.

> *Our world requires change if it is going to survive.*
> *I am talking about the planet herself and also mankind.*
> *The destitute conditions of our planet and our intolerance of one another*
> *are sure signs that the time has arrived for each of us to embrace our Goddess within.*
> – DR. KATHRYN MORAVIA, PhD –

MOST WOMEN ARE AWARE OF THE GODDESS ARCHETYPES that have existed throughout the ages. There are many wonderful books describing in great detail the world as it existed in many diverse cultures when the Goddess was worshipped as part of daily spiritual practice.

In the book *Goddesses in Everywoman*, Dr. Jean Shinoda Bolen says, "All the goddesses are potential patterns in the psyches of all women, yet in each individual woman some of these patterns are activated (energized or developed) and others are not." Throughout our lives we express different aspects of these archetypes to reflect our inner yearnings.

As we flow with the feminine energy within ourselves, we can move with relative ease from being the independent Athena, to the centered Hestia, to the charming Aphrodite, depending how open our hearts are.

According to Bolen, "the child's inherent goddess pattern interacts with family expectations. If the family disapproves of the specific goddess, however, a girl doesn't stop feeling the way she does, although she may learn not to act naturally, and her self-esteem suffers." To comply with the wishes of others, we have all shut down aspects of ourselves that longed to be expressed. Historically, however, this has not served us well.

Archeological discoveries after World War II show evidence of a peaceful, remarkably advanced prehistoric agricultural society where the Goddess was worshiped extensively, and where women and men lived in harmony. Neither sex dominated the other, but each shared natural skills and abilities. As futurist writers John Naisbitt and Patricia Aburdene share in their book *Megatrends for Women*, this civilization extended across Turkey and into the Middle East, as far west as France and as far north as Poland.

History books are filled with stories describing a 500-year period when throughout much of Europe women with ancient knowledge were tortured and burned at the stake, accused of being witches. During these dark times women who had been healers, midwives and herbalists — women with knowledge — were "quieted" as Christianity gained acceptance. Only men were allowed to practice medicine, and the innate qualities of the feminine were devalued and seen as troublesome or evil.

We've come a long way since those dark times. Ancient knowledge is now experiencing a resurrection amongst women. However, there is still a lot of work to be done. Acceptance of the masculine as the ideal way to run our world has led to the misuse of power and control and created terrible imbalances across the planet. Old habits die hard. Old ideas are slow to change. Unfortunately, our dear Mother Earth doesn't have much of a future if we don't take it upon ourselves to once again express our feminine power. This power is of a higher form. It does not consist of having power "over" another person, place or thing. This is the power that comes with opening our hearts to love. The power comes through us — healing, helping and harmonizing with all aspects of life.

This is a real shift in our current reality, but one that is sorely needed, now. The injustices that women have suffered in the past, and continue to experience, affect us all. Because we are all one, when one of our sisters suffers, we all suffer. We can choose to sit quietly on the sidelines and whine, to suffer in silence, or to take action.

That action is love — love in action.

Musings & Blessings

A T A CELLULAR LEVEL WE ARE PART OF THE WOMEN who have passed before us — our great, great, great grandmother's mothers, sisters and aunts.

When do you find yourself most distressed about the past injustices women have endured throughout time? What do you do to heal yourself from that pain and suffering? When you have your period, do you feel particularly vulnerable to the suffering of others? How can you make a difference by looking after yourself during this time? What can you do to alleviate the pain and suffering of another? Go inside and feel in your body what you can do, and then do it!

Your feminine sexual essence is waiting to be expressed, so that you may better serve yourself and others. Find ways to honor and respect yourself.

You have to do what you love to do,
not get stuck in that comfort zone of a regular life.
Life is not a dress rehearsal. This is it.
— LUCINDA BASSETT —

Feminine Sexual Essence

My Darling Feminine Heart:

Sometimes I get so very tired.
Not only does my body ache, but my heart aches too.
Of course I can do it all, or at least I will try.
But when I have to embrace my Brave Heart so often
I feel that my Feminine Heart suffers.
That beautiful and fragrant flower that resides within me
starts to wither, and you don't notice me anymore,
I hardly recognize myself.
Then my heart cracks …
and the love comes seeping in.
My true love is once again at home.
My body, heart and soul radiates with love.
Thank you, Goddess,
the divine feminine.

With or without a man, you can practice opening your body to flow
with pleasure, while opening your heart as an offering of love's yearning.
— DAVID DEIDA —

AS HUMAN BEINGS WE HAVE BOTH MASCULINE AND FEMININE ASPECTS, because physically we have varying amounts of both sex hormones. If we are born into a female body, it is our destiny to express our radiant feminine energy. Some men exhibit more feminine qualities than masculine, and some women have more masculine qualities. These qualities are affected at birth and are influenced by our social environment. Both masculine and feminine qualities have important roles to play in creating new life, and we need them both.

If it wasn't for masculine energy, little would be accomplished on this planet. Purpose of action and a focus on accomplishment are masculine qualities. It goes against the grain for a woman with a strong feminine sexual essence to be a goal-setter and go-getter. She would much rather delight in nature, laugh in love, and follow her emotional tides as they roll in and out of her day.

We are all children of Mother Earth. As we move into the 21st century, we have become very aware of people's sexual natures, and of couples who do not fit into the traditional roles of masculine and feminine. Canada has led the world in legalizing same-sex marriages, something that people in many countries are still grappling with. We are recognizing that our sexual essence is more than just our physical bodies.

The average overworked, overstressed and overwhelmed woman feels unsupported. The never-ending daily tasks that need to be done weigh heavily on her, and inside she feels split. She can embrace her masculine qualities of goal-setting and accomplishment and get everything done, or she can breathe in her feminine essence occasionally and try to get back into her feminine body, mind and Spirit.

David Deida, in his pioneering book *Intimate Communion: Awakening Your Sexual Essence*, says, "The Feminine force is much more than womanhood. The Feminine is the force of life itself, and you can experience it in many ways."

Many women have invested so heavily in identifying with their masculine aspects that they have forgotten their feminine essence, or neatly tucked it away for a later date.

As women, most of us enjoy the freedom of having our own earning power, of being able to provide for ourselves and for others. It makes us feel proud, worthwhile and independent. We've become pretty good at it, too.

Yet we suffer. When we don't take the time to nurture our feminine essence, we pay a price. Through the sighs and tears, we do it all ourselves. Single women and single mothers are especially at risk of sadness and burnout, as they don't have the helping hand of a partner, someone to share responsibilities with or to provide a strong shoulder to sop up tears.

Many enlightened women in all spheres of life are accomplished in their fields, and I have utmost respect for them. I have had my own goals and successes. I know what it takes to shepherd projects from idea or dream through to completion.

When a woman is not able to access her femininity easily, her suffering becomes intolerable. Research shows that as we inch toward middle age, the sadness and suffering starts to eat away at us, affecting not only our spiritual radiance, but our physical bodies as well. Stress compromises our immune systems, often resulting in early aging, arthritis and even the onset of cancer.

Unable to surrender to the deep love and connection with others, the Feminine Heart starts to feel ripped off. We start asking, "Is this all there is? I am accomplished in the outer world, yet my inner world is suffering and slowly dying. The sweet nectar of happiness is not available — and there certainly isn't any joy, let alone ecstasy!"

We hunger to connect deeply with our own Spirit. We long to be felt and understood by others, especially by the opposite sex, for who we really are — physically, emotionally and spiritually. We desire to be seen for who we really are, and to show and share our radiance.

Like a magnet to metal, for attraction to take place there needs to be polarity. Even in same-sex coupling, one partner adopts a more masculine role. Energy must be balanced. As our relationships go through the ebb and flow of life we change, taking on more or less of the opposite sexual energy. When we take on too much masculine energy we lose out, and so does everybody else.

Constantly moving and changing, the Feminine Heart is able to express the full experience of life. She can shift from a night-blooming jasmine, sitting delicately on a branch just being the beauty that it is, to the raging waves of a stormy sea. Archetypal, innate feminine gifts are not always as sweet as a mother's nurturing hug, or the understanding compassion of a girlfriend. Feminine energy can be just as ferocious as the most terrifying animal. When required, the Feminine Heart possesses superhuman strength. Like the wrath of nature herself, her wildness and fierceness when she has been threatened, betrayed or abused can stir fear in the hearts of the bravest men.

An old saying, "Hell hath no fury like a woman scorned," captures this ferocity of the feminine Spirit. A lioness protecting her vulnerable kittens at the moment of possible danger fears nothing. The feminine Spirit is no different when she must protect herself or her loved ones. Like the fury of the wildest storm, when she unleashes her anger the relentless typhoon of the feminine Spirit can destroy anything in her path.

Like the Hindu deity Kali, who gives and takes away, a dark and wrathful face exists within us, well-hidden behind the sweetness of a passionate kiss. If not treated with respect, she comes out to tear off the head of her enemy and drink its blood. This potential of Kali exists within us all. Bless those who encounter her wrath.

IN MY EARLY 20S I TRAVELED AROUND GUATEMALA en route to South America to participate in the *Festival of the Sun* in Peru. This ancient festival of the Incas takes place every hundred years, and I was curious to experience the festivities of a culture that had long captivated my interest. I had already traveled alone to many places far away from my small prairie hometown in northern Canada, and I considered myself a seasoned traveler.

For all my meanderings and adventures, however, I was still innocent, trusting and fairly naïve. Having grown up in a traditional family, my father had taught us to live by the golden rule: "Do unto others as you would have them do unto you." He never warned me that sometimes people would try to do things to me that I couldn't even conceive.

I rented a small cottage outside the hippy town of Panajachel along the Gringo trail of Central America. Everybody passed through there on the journey to South America. There was no electricity, but it was new and clean. Some of the more enterprising locals had built simple restaurants and hotels that catered to traveling youth. In the evenings I would get a little bored or lonely, and one night I decided to walk into town for some social stimulation and a nice meal.

It was dusk, and the colors along the dusty path captured my imagination. A pink and golden light fell gently as I followed the winding trail. Preoccupied with thoughts of the delicious meal ahead, I walked quickly in anticipation.

Suddenly, a stocky Indian man dressed in full traditional garb appeared out of nowhere. Another man rushed me from the other side. In an instant they locked onto my hands, pulling me off the trail. I didn't have time to react. I didn't even think about struggling or fighting. I couldn't.

For a split second my body went stiff, and my mind went blank. Then I felt this incredible wave of energy rise up through the ground into my feet and go shooting out the top of my head. It was like an electrical surge. Everything went blank for a second, and then the power came pouring back in.

In the split second when my body went stiff, I felt my power leave. Then the force that surged back in took control of my mind, my body and my spirit. This incredible force entered my lungs, filling my chest like a balloon about to burst, and out came the terrifying roar of a ferocious lioness protecting her young.

When I saw the men running away, I realized that the sound had come out of me. Terrified of the animal I had just encountered, I stood there shaking and sobbing. What had just happened? Where did that sound come from? Did that animal live inside me?

Everything had happened so quickly. I wasn't sure how to explain it. But to this day I am fully aware of the ferocious aspect of the feminine. I know that when needed she is available to serve and protect.

If we are to make big changes on the planet, there will be times when we must access this aspect of the feminine. It takes courage and heart. Alone and together, we must share all aspects of the divine feminine essence to most quickly and positively impact our world.

Musings & Blessings

WHAT CAN WE DO TO GET OUT OF OUR HEADS and back into our bodies to reconnect with our Feminine Hearts? Many of us reach for chocolate — or sweet, rich velvety ice cream — and lots of it! That works, momentarily. Options with fewer calories include going for a soothing massage, or taking a leisurely bubble bath. Try getting out into nature and notice the beauty that is everywhere. If you deeply connect with nature, breathing in her magnificence, you, too, will become fulfilled. Most important, don't forget to breathe in the love that is all around, and to exhale anything that doesn't feel like love. Ahhhh … feel better already?

As you breathe in deeply, take in all the love that is in and around you, and smile.

They will follow the Lord, he will roar like a lion.
When he roars, his children will come trembling from the west.
– HOSEA 11:10 –
(from *The Chronicles of Narnia*)

Spiritually Enlightened Women

My Darling Feminine Heart:

I know that I have come
from a long line of wise women
who served the needs of the world during their time.
But we now live in different times.
My heart is aware that the greatest service
I can offer the world now
is sharing my spiritual wisdom.
My soul yearns to quell
the cries coming from the darkness of fear.
Thank you, Goddess, for making me a messenger
of your love and light.

> *There came a time when the risk to remain tight in a bud*
> *was more painful than it took to blossom.*
> – ANAIS NIN –

SINCE THE 1960S WOMEN EN MASSE have started questioning their roles. We knew that we didn't want to step in our mothers' footprints — they didn't have a lot of choices. Many of the women who came before us had to rely upon men for economic survival. So we got an education, so we could get a good job, so we would be financially independent, so we wouldn't have to rely on a man.

Women today have entered every facet of industry and business. But the industrialized world is a different place than it was forty years ago. We have evolved. In breaking through the shackles of limitation to gain independence, we discovered that our heart's deepest expression suffers. By opening our hearts to our deepest truth, we became spiritually conscious. We acknowledged that our greatest gifts were being in service to others. This service was not out of duty, as in the past, but from a much higher place. We have an inner knowing that we have much to offer that can make a difference to the state of the planet.

We've had to look critically at our roles, and we've made a sociological shift. We are once again willing to embrace more of our innate feminine traits, to become the kinds of leaders and caretakers that the world now requires. We can have it all — just not all at the same time.

Although it was in the 1960s that women started to question their role in society, most men didn't start reviewing their role until the early 1980s. Twenty-odd years later, as a backlash to the feminist movement, men started looking at their traditional role as providers and leaders. As women started climbing higher and higher rungs on corporate ladders, men started wearing their hair longer, putting on more jewelry and wearing pastel colors. Today, both men and women have evolved beyond the survival mode of our parents, and have started embracing all aspects of both the masculine and the feminine.

A S WE JOURNEY THROUGH THE STAGES OF WOMANHOOD we become aware of the changes in our bodies. Every month it is obvious that our bodies have a life of their own, a life that cannot be controlled by our will. Some women wish that their monthly periods didn't come, but come they do. We begin to realize that we are not just our bodies, and we are not just our minds. At some point, we also realize that we are connected to something much bigger than both of these things.

Every month we have a reminder that we have a connection with a creative life force. As we grow in our awareness and wisdom, we cannot deny that we are indeed one with all life.

In *The Power of Now*, author Eckhart Tolle suggests that women are potentially closer to enlightenment than men because it is easier for women to feel and be in their bodies, so they are naturally closer to "being."

Once a woman has been satiated by this fullness of being, she will never forget the taste. Throughout her life she may try to get back that sublime flavor of deep intimacy – filling herself with food, buying another pair of shoes, starting a new romance. But nothing tastes as good as being connected to our Higher

Self feels. These appetizing distractions may take the edge off her hunger, but they will never give her the deep sense of satisfaction she craves.

... nothing tastes as good as being connected to our Higher Self feels.

We can spend a lifetime looking for things or ways to give us that feeling of being filled up. Ultimately, in our wisdom, we realize that fulfillment comes from feeding the deepest need of our Feminine Hearts — giving and receiving love. When we have our hearts broken or trampled on we evaluate our situations and we hash things out with our girlfriends (our own best therapists). Protecting our hearts from more pain we build shells around them, then we go and cry with our friends, or we go to a therapist. Hopefully we are able to work through our issues, and find the strength to surrender our hearts so that they may open up once again.

Men don't have that same luxury. On their own, men are slower to work through healing. As women, we are naturally more aware of our emotional world. Men tend to be at a disadvantage in this department. Don't get me wrong — many highly developed and spiritually aware men are out there. But in my experience, the number of men who have embraced their spiritual side does not equal the number of women. But they are working on it.

Instead of complaining about the lack of spiritually aware men, however, we can be leaders. We can actually help a man move out of his head and into his heart. When a man senses that he is in the presence of a woman who he can trust, he will start opening his heart up to her. That is a really good place for the Masculine to start feeling his connection to Spirit. This is one of the greatest gifts we can give a man, helping him to feel and open his heart to life.

"I can't be bothered to train another man," a sophisticated, middle-aged matchmaking client told me frankly. "If a man isn't already on the spiritual path, I am not interested in meeting with him."

I had heard this comment many times before, and I clearly understood her concerns. The unfortunate aspect to this attitude is that it is all about "what can I get," instead of "what do I have to offer." This adjustment in our approach can make a huge difference in the numbers of men available for a spiritual partnership.

The armor around a man's heart may not yet have cracked open — but as an enlightened woman, this is your gift. Using your feminine essence, you carry the key to open the heart of any man graced by your presence. I highly suggest blessing the people in your life and at the same time fulfilling your heart's desire.

Spirit is calling the Feminine Heart more loudly than ever before, because our dear Mother Earth and her children need us more than they ever have. We can choose to ignore her plaintive cry but we suffer deeply — like hearing our own children cry out for help — if we do not heed the call.

Musings & Blessings

How can you be more aware of the presence of Spirit in your everyday life? How often during the day, the hour or the minute do you acknowledge that you are a divine Spirit? To live from that place of awareness may take practice. To manifest Spirit, treat every day like Christmas day. Make life a celebration of love and gratitude for the heart of Goddess is everywhere.

What lightens your heart and fills your soul with wonder? Find something or somebody you love. Immerse yourself in the beauty and wonder of that feeling of love. Relax into your Feminine Heart, breathing through any constrictions. Exhale, releasing everything that doesn't serve your highest good. While you are breathing, smell your surroundings and take in the sweet nectar around you. Exhale, again; relax your mind and let your body express the love in and around you. We have an inner knowing of that part of our destiny. The opportunities to do so are endless.

Breathe deeply. The love we feel in our hearts is the fertile soil in which we plant our seeds of creativity.

We must cultivate our garden.
— Voltaire —

The Light Workers

My Darling Feminine Heart:

We do not need to feel alone anymore,
because we are not.
They come in every shape and size.
Age is of no consequence.
As long as we are mindful not to judge
they are waiting to join with us.
Standing in line at the supermarket with her boisterous child in tow,
I catch her eyes and see her radiant light.
I can feel the world of love inside her.
She sees me too.
I nod, smiling, and she smiles back.
She recognizes me.
She is one of us.

Life begets life. Energy creates energy.
It is by spending oneself that one becomes rich.
— SARAH BERNHARDT —

MANY ENLIGHTENED WOMEN ON THE PLANET KNOW that they are here to heal others, and to heal Mother Earth. These women come in all kinds of packages. They don't physically resemble one another except for one distinguishing factor — these women are all filled with the radiant love and light of our Creator.

These people choose to share the light in their daily lives by being in service to others. We can find them everywhere that healing is taking place. They are the "earth angels" whose purpose it is to help shape the destiny of our planet.

They have a big job, but they are up to it. I call these open-hearted creatures the light workers.

An increasing number of people — appearing in both the masculine and feminine physical form — are feeling the pull of their higher destinies during this time of the earth's evolution. Their destiny craves to express itself in a way that serves as a contribution to the healing of the planet. And in their own quiet way, they are making inroads.

The light workers are bringing light into every facet of society. We work in schools, hospitals, governments and at home. We are the living embodiment of love, and we share that grace wherever we go. The light workers have an enormous task — to light up the darkness on this planet. No easy task to be sure.

Part of the job description of the light worker is to take a stand for peace by using love as a weapon for creation, not destruction. "Love bombing," is part of the job description. We know that violence and warfare is creating darkness in the lives of billions of people. We are spiritual warriors, intentionally shedding light on this darkness. But we bomb with love instead of hate, jealousy and fear.

I like to love bomb the elderly. The elderly are so undervalued in Western society, yet they have so much to offer. Often they live alone or with their spouse, as their families have moved away. Sometimes their families are too busy to visit them. Often after they have lost a spouse they have no one to talk to. Because the feminine enjoys relating so much, many older women will make an effort to form friendships, or to keep in contact with others, but many men are isolated.

When I am out and about during the day, I often smile my biggest smile and say warm hellos to old gentlemen as they shuffle down the street. Often they are taken aback. Sometimes they stop in their tracks, smiling back. What my small act of kindness says is this: "I see you, and I acknowledge you. I hope that your day is as wonderful as you are."

We may never know the impact of the love we so freely give. It may have saved a person's life. Or it may have been passed on to another, quite unintentionally. Love is an energy that only transforms — it is never destroyed.

Children also need our love and light. Young children are very aware of energy. Like animals, they can pick up on your energy without you having to say or do anything. They can just feel you.

One day I was walking through a business center where there was a daycare. A young woman was pushing a huge stroller with about five toddlers strapped into their seats. As I walked past, I used my intention to connect with these earth angels. With my heart open, I consciously sent them love. With their receptive hearts, they easily and instantaneously picked up on my love. As I passed, they all turned around and stared at me. I looked each one in the eyes, sending this message: "You are an earth angel, a child of our Creator living on this earth."

"Yes, we know," they answered, looking back at me with sparkling clear eyes.

Not a word was shared between me and this bevy of earth angels, but we communicated with our love. We acknowledged each other as children of the earth. I think that on some level, this could heal them. Or it could help them heal another person, especially when they share their big, uncensored, innocent smiles of love.

We were filled with love and light when we came into this life. Depending on our early environments and experiences, some of us have shut down our radiant hearts as a means of protection. Without a concerted effort, many adults never reconnect with that divine aspect of themselves.

Many of the children born on the planet over the last 10 years or so are filled with this light. They know what their purpose is. They are called "indigo children" or "crystal kids" because of their high vibrations. Research shows that they exhibit many of the symptoms of children labeled with ADD or ADHD. These enlightened yet often misunderstood individuals have a definite purpose — to help heal our planet. Make sure that your children are not being medicated with something they don't need. If you have any concerns about your child's predisposition, do your homework before you fill any prescriptions.

Musings & Blessings

OUR CONTRIBUTIONS AS LIGHT WORKERS and sharers of love are blessings that are ours to be celebrated and shared. When you misuse or forget your purpose you will start judging others, stop sharing your light and add more fear to this fear-filled world. If you find yourself in such activities – stop! You know better. Allowing your Feminine Heart to shrink and your light to diminish is no alternative. You will be limiting your potential for healing and growing.

Who can you find who can mirror your radiant love back to you? Sometimes we need a gentle reminder of who we came here to be. That's what friends are for. Share your light with your brothers and sisters and they will mirror it back to you. Give each other your special essence. Bless each other with that sweet nectar. If you would like to give a gift of love to another person, what would that look like?

What is your deepest purpose? How can you express it while offering your Feminine Heart? How are you going to share it?

Breathe in deeply with the intention of letting in the answer. Breathe out, exhaling anything that doesn't support your dreams to come true. Breathe in love.

We are always in choice. Either we can bring more light into the world, or we can keep it to ourselves. The latter is not an alternative for the enlightened woman.

Nothing can resist the human will that will stake
even its existence on its stated purpose.
– Benjamin Disraeli –

The Power of Feminine Thought

My Darling Feminine Heart:

I thought I was hurt
and my pain became intolerable.
I thought I was betrayed
and my heart went cold.
I allowed myself to lose hope
and felt myself dying.
Then I thought about you …
my thoughts changed.
I thought about the love
that waited patiently within my heart,
and it came out to play with me.
Then all I could think about
was the power of my thoughts.
Thank you, Goddess, for showing me
that what I think about
I bring about.

The game of life is the game of boomerangs.
Our thoughts, deeds and words return to us, sooner or later, with astounding accuracy.
— FLORENCE SCOVEL SHINN —

To PARAPHRASE AN ANCIENT EASTERN TEACHING: Our thoughts become our words, our words become our actions, our actions become our habits, and our habits create our lives.

When we take an honest look at our lives, we can see how our thoughts have created our reality. We are literally what we think. Our lives mirror our thoughts. This is true whether we feel out of sync with our surroundings, or blessed by them. As we grow, our circumstances evolve. As we become more aware of our thoughts and we learn to practice self-control, we notice how our circumstances shift in direct ratio with our altered awareness.

We cannot have love without giving it away, and we cannot give it away if we don't have it.

Every woman decides at some point that her life will be a certain way; that her life will go down a certain path. Sometimes she consciously chooses the path but if not, the path chooses her. Circumstances happen beyond her control. It is her thoughts about the situation that affect the outcome. Something happens, and she reacts to the experience. Whether this reaction is anger, frustration or sadness, the first step is to acknowledge the feeling. The next step is to embrace it. After embracing the emotion, it must be dissolved, which requires keeping her heart open.

Focus on the love that is within us and available at all times. We must give away the love that we so deeply crave. We must open our hearts to receive the love that we give so freely. It is all one. We cannot have love without giving it away, and we cannot give it away if we don't have it.

I CHOSE MY LIFE PATH AT FOUR YEARS OF AGE. It was the winter of 1960, and I remember the snow banks at the side of the road were higher than I was. Living in northern Saskatchewan in the winter makes one strong and hard.

My father was a trainman for the Canadian National Railway, and work that winter was sporadic. They called you when they needed you, and you were grateful for the work.

One gray afternoon the call came for my father to go back to work. Although I wasn't aware of it at the time, many of the men employed by the CNR spent time commiserating at one of the local bars, drinking beer to pass away the long, cold days. This particular afternoon, my father was at the bar with his buddies.

I could tell from my mother's sense of urgency that this was an important call. She needed to contact my father so that he could respond to his call for work. For some reason my mother was not able to call him by phone, so we headed down to the bar. In those days there were no cell phones, and my mother did not have a driver's license. She had to walk. We lived in a small city, and the bar was about 30 minutes away.

I remember the look of determination on my mother's face as she bundled my younger sister and me into our snowsuits "because we had to go get Daddy." We started off from the house, both my sister and I piled onto an old sleigh. My mother's steps were brisk as she pulled us over the crisp white snow, the January wind blowing around us. Even at this early age, I remember feeling a strange sense of vulnerability and anger that my mother had to make this trek with us in tow.

After several blocks my mother asked me to walk, as she was getting tired from pulling. Her arms ached — my sister and I were small, but heavy, bundles. I remember trudging along beside her, wondering what we were doing. We finally arrived at the door of the bar. I expected that we would go in, get my father, and warm up.

My mother stood at the door and waited.

"Let's go in," I suggested.

"We can't," my mother replied.

"Why not?" I asked, confused. We had walked all this way to get my father, and it seemed natural that we would go in to get him. We had finally arrived at the place where he was supposed to be, and we were not going in to get him! I didn't understand.

"See this sign?" my mother said, sadly. I couldn't read yet, so she pointed to the words and read them out slowly, "No Women or Minors Allowed."

"What's a minor?" I asked, quizzically.

My mother explained that there were rules that had to be obeyed regarding how old you had to be to enter a beer parlor, which I vaguely understood. I couldn't understand why my mother was not allowed to go in to this building to get my father so that he could go to work. Even at that young age, I remember how indignant I was.

I was starting to get cold, very cold. After working up a sweat from walking so far in my big snowsuit my body had cooled down, and now I was freezing. My little sister, who was still sitting in the sleigh, started to cry. I could see the look of helplessness on my mother's face.

"We'll just wait until someone comes out and ask him to go and get your father," she said, trying to sound cheerful.

I wasn't convinced. This did not make sense. How could my mother, who I knew to be a strong and capable person, be so weak? Why didn't she just go in there and get my father herself?

We stood there for what seemed like forever, although it was probably only 10 or 15 minutes, until a young man came staggering outside. The urgency in my mother's voice as she explained the situation left the man no choice but to go back inside and retrieve my father.

Shortly afterward my father came out, looking surprised. My mother explained the situation. He told us to go home and that he would be along shortly.

Trudging back through the snow, I remember making some decisions about the future of my life. I decided that I would do whatever I could to make sure I would always be treated as well as any man and never would I allow myself to feel less important or powerful as a human being because I was a girl. This was the beginning of my life story, the point at which I decided to take care of myself.

Sometimes situations that happen early in life can profoundly affect us for years. We then create stories from our past, through which we filter all our subsequent experiences. It takes awareness to see these stories from out past, and courage to create new, self-affirming stories to live by.

I BECAME VERY GOOD AT LOOKING AFTER MYSELF and projecting that I was so independent that I did not need a man; but it has not served my Feminine Heart. Throughout my life, experiences with other men compounded my belief about being able to rely on them. It took me years of personal growth work to allow myself to surrender to a deserving man, and to allow the abundant flow of the universe to enter my life. My healing started when I was able to forgive my father. He did the best he could at the time, in his own evolution.

Most women have similar stories hidden deep inside, of men who have disappointed, hurt or betrayed them. When this happens, we see all our experiences with men through the filters we have chosen to protect ourselves. This creates very unsatisfying possibilities for relationships with men.

Old stories die hard. Yet in the end, we have the power to change how we relate to the story. This takes conscious effort and awareness. Awareness is half the battle. With it, we can choose who we are in the present, and not let the past affect our future.

Negativity is pervasive in our culture. When circumstances are challenging, the easy way out is to blame outside forces, making us feel victimized. We focus on the negatives, losing ourselves in the 'problem.' We point to our unhappy circumstances to rationalize our negative feelings. This is the easy way out. It takes very little effort to feel like a victim.

In her book *The Dark Side of the Light Chasers*, author Debbie Ford says, "The key is to understand that there is nothing we can see or perceive that we are not. If we did not possess a certain quality, we would not recognize it in another. Being part of the holographic world, we are all that we see, all that we judge, all that we admire."

We do not attract that which we want, but that which we are. Our lives are like computers, and we have the programs that we install in them. Input negative thoughts and actions, and negativity will show up on your screen of life. Input love, kindness and grace, and your life's circumstances will download those programs as well.

We do not attract that which we want, but that which we are.

To best serve our Feminine Hearts we need to fill our minds daily with loving and empowering visions for our life, and for the lives of others. Keeping our loving hearts open, and our thoughts centered on a vision for the world that is empowering, loving and peace-filled, will do wonders to affect the changes that are possible for the future of our world.

We can do many simple things to eliminate the negative thoughts that are pervasive in our culture. For the sensitive Feminine Heart, watching the late-night news might not be as helpful as listening to relaxing music or reading a captivating novel before going to sleep. Carrying visions of pain, destruction and despair into bed as we let go of our last minutes of consciousness is not a positive way to enter the dreamland of our unconscious.

In the book *Conscious Evolution*, author Barbara Marx Hubbard suggests that a television show be created called the *NewNews: What's Working in the World*. Hubbard describes this potential program as a megaphone for creative breakthroughs and successes, as a real "tell-a-vision" inviting people to participate in constructive action. This kind of programming could be used to plant the seeds of possibilities in our minds; seeds that germinate while we are in deep slumber.

Women with highly developed perceptive abilities feel the vibrations of what is happening in their physical bodies, and what is happening in the "body" of Mother Earth. Intuitively, we feel the pain and suffering of others. It is important to stay current with what is affecting life on the planet, but during the special time just before falling asleep it is important to input thoughts of gratitude. We must be grateful for all the ways we can give and receive love. That is part of our job description, as the feminine life force on the planet.

We don't always have control over what happens to us, but we do have control about how we respond to the situation. Accepting responsibility for our thoughts, feelings and actions keeps us in our power. Take the responsibility for rewriting the endings to your own stories. Write powerful endings that allow you to move forward in your full wisdom and grace.

At some point, a woman realizes what gives her the most joy. We look outside ourselves for what we want. We look to other people to love us and to give our lives value and meaning, but nobody can do this for us. We must do this for ourselves. We can't look to others to remind us that we are children of Mother Earth, radiant beings of light and Goddesses of good. We are the planet's earth angels. It doesn't matter what other people would have us believe. We are the only ones who can give ourselves permission to be the beauty that we are.

Musings & Blessings

Looking back over the course of your life, what old stories are you still playing out? Are these stories empowering or debilitating? What has happened in the past that makes you feel victimized? What are some of the old stories from your past that are affecting your future?

Allowing your past life stories to hold you in the grip of old myths doesn't serve your highest learning. Acknowledge your feelings surrounding the experience; blessing all those who hurt or betrayed you. Find your heart center, breathe in love, and forgive them. They were doing their best, according to their own evolution. With Spirit as your guide, choose the best ending for your own story, and then find the forgiveness to release the hurt or pain.

If you are having trouble letting go of debilitating scripts you have written for yourself, you may want to share your story with a friend or a qualified professional. Ask for help in releasing any pain you hold in your heart. You can rewrite the myth you have created, too. Then you have the freedom to change how you want the story to end.

Do you feel that you are freely sharing your radiant light? Are you living as a part-time or full-time light worker? It matters not. The only important thing is to breathe in love and light, exhaling fear and restrictions. That is all you have to "do."

The more we become aware of the power of our thoughts, the more power we have to create a life where we can make a difference not only in our own lives, but in the lives of others as well.

Remember that there is only one difference between an ordinary woman
and an extraordinary woman: The belief that she is ordinary.
— FAWN GERMER —

Women Today

My Darling Feminine Heart:

I am tired of fighting for something
that I know was always mine.
My personal power
is something I must give to myself
not wait for outside forces
to give it to me.
Instead of fighting, I will rest.
I will share the gifts and blessings
I have always had to offer.
Thank you, Goddess, for helping me to relax,
knowing it is all perfection.

I am a woman, above everything else.
— JACQUELINE KENNEDY ONASSIS —

THE WORLD HAS CHANGED AND WE, as women, have evolved. The last 40 years have seen women's roles change significantly, and we have either led or responded to these changes. Although we have taken our hits along the way, with few role models to follow we've blazed new paths. Living in the industrialized world, we have many options and freedoms that the majority of the women on this planet do not have.

But many women today have also forgotten how to connect with their timeless feminine wisdom. This wisdom is not sufficiently rewarded or acknowledged as a viable commodity in today's marketplace, so we've swept it under the proverbial musty old rug. We've been so busy trying to compete with men, and to be their equals, that we have lost the very essence of what it means to be feminine.

Not for one instant do I suggest that women were better off before the strides of feminism brought us onto a more equal playing field with men. With these inroads however, we have made sacrifices that don't serve the Feminine Heart. Many modern women have given up so much of their natural feminine essence that they feel dissatisfied with their lives.

What the world needs now are women who don't strive to be equals among men, but women who are willing to authentically claim their feminine essence. That is what will heal the ills of our planet and at the same time heal the relationships between men and women.

I can hear the howls of feminists around the world, upset because we have worked so hard for what we have attained. But the time has come for us to move beyond the ideals of feminism. We know in our hearts that we are not just equal to men, we have been given our own gifts to share with the world. Moving beyond feminism, we are entering the age of post-feminism where we no longer have to compete or prove ourselves. Our greatest offering now is to share all those gifts that we have neglected for so long.

The Feminine Heart intuitively understands that she is connected with Spirit, and that Spirit is life itself. When we deny ourselves that loving connection with the creative life force that resides within, we suffer. When we suffer, we are adding to the negativity on the planet.

Living in a world where masculine energy is the source of intention and action, we have embraced those aspects of ourselves while ignoring or downplaying our feminine gifts. How can we access our feminine sexual essence easily while continuing to live our daily lives in a predominantly masculine culture?

Sharing the unlimited love of our Feminine Hearts, we create meaningful lives for ourselves. Working together, we can co-create the possibility of a new world order. When we go inside to that place of inner knowing, we will be connected to the creative Spirit of life, and once again, we can live in harmony with ourselves and with others. Not only will we feel more blessed, but our children and the generations to come will be gifted by our thoughts and actions now.

"But I am so busy," you are thinking. "I don't have time to do anything else."

We live our lives as a race — as somewhere to get to. We are so busy running from one activity to the next that we often miss the journey between the destinations. Did you ever get to the point where it was hip to be busy? "Let me see, I've got to check my day timer. Oh, no that won't work, how about the week after that? I have a little time in the afternoon on Wednesday." Does this sound familiar to you?

Women always talk about how busy they are. It is a badge of honor, and we wear it with pride. We have adopted this mantra, as though "busyness" was next to godliness. We are so busy running after the next thing that we rarely have time to just be in the now. However, the only place we have any power and deep fulfillment is in the now. Sure, dreams and hopes are a wonderful part of life. But the present moment is what gives us the juice of life.

The Feminine Heart does not respond well to constantly running behind the clock, or to living according to a day-timer. Day after day and year after year of this race without a finish line wears the Feminine Heart down. It doesn't take long before the radiant light and beauty of her youth is snuffed out, and she becomes a dull shell of her former self.

The most common complaint I hear from women in my work is that they don't have enough quality time for themselves, let alone time for the people that they most love — their family and friends. Try to squeeze some time in for community or volunteer work, and something has to give. Usually what gives is inner peace — the connection with our own inner truth. Many of us do not take the time to listen to that quiet voice inside that is the guiding light for ourselves and the people we care about.

"Why has time disappeared in our culture?" asks author and philosopher Jacob Needleman. "How is it that after decades of inventions and new technologies devoted to saving time and labor, the result is that there is no time left? We are a time-poor society; we are temporally impoverished. And there is no issue, no aspect of human life that exceeds this in importance. The destruction of time is literally the destruction of life."

New research suggests that even when women are the major wage earners in the family, they still do the bulk of the work around the house. Don't forget all the household holiday preparations and shopping, shuffling children to events, coordinating doctors and school appointments, all the household cleaning and putting away... and the list goes on. Yes, some men take on some of these responsibilities, but women still do the vast majority of the domestic labor, no matter how much they contribute to the family's financial bottom line.

This has stretched many women beyond their capacity to follow their flowing Feminine Hearts. To keep up in the workplace women have given up much of themselves, but they are running so fast on the treadmill that it is difficult to jump off. They don't dare go inside to feel their hearts, for fear of the pain and emptiness that will meet them there.

For this state of affairs, we have no one to blame but ourselves. We have forgotten who we are, and what our true purpose is. We have let time, or the lack thereof, rule our lives. There is, however, nothing more you need to do to experience a sense of peace in your life. It is who you are *being*, while you are busy *doing* your life, that will create a different understanding of time.

Not only should you give love freely, but you should also do what you can to be a peacemaker. Wherever you go, bring your radiant calmness, harmony and love with you. No one wants to be around negative energy. When you are negative, everyone will avoid you. Be intentional about becoming positive. Create a habit of it.

Musings & Blessings

TAKE A MOMENT AND INHALE DEEPLY, letting go of any tension in your body as you exhale. Close your eyes and go inside. Listen to your body. Listen to your thoughts. Listen to your Spirit. When you are still, you will hear the sweet song of love calling your name. Love is all there is. Give thanks. You are in the now. Reflect on the following questions:

How much of your day do you spend in activities or thoughts that don't contribute to your well-being, or to the well-being of those around you? Every night before going to sleep ask yourself, "Was I living my truth today? Did I live my intentions? What could I have done differently?" Breathe in deeply and acknowledge yourself for doing the best you could, for today. As you exhale, forgive yourself for any shortcomings that you may feel about yourself.

Give thanks to our Creator, and the next day incorporate some of those things into your day. Within a short time you will feel lighter, happier and fulfilled as you start to embrace a life that is more authentically yours.

To live is so startling it leaves little time for anything else.
— EMILY DICKINSON —

The Myth of Having it All

My Darling Feminine Heart:

I've tried my best
to have it all
by doing it all.
Lover, mother, friend,
cook, gardener, interior decorator, caregiver
cleaner, launderer, nurse, therapist…
The list never ends.
They told me that I could
be everything to everyone
and I believed them.
Now that I've done it all
there's not much left for me.
Thank you, dear Goddess, for showing me
there is nothing I need to have.
All I need to do, is be.

Be not anxious about what you have, but about what you are.
— POPE GREGORY I —

HAVING IT ALL HAS BECOME A UBIQUITOUS CATCHPHRASE with modern women everywhere in the free world. From Singapore to Iceland, the advertising and marketing pundits would have us believe that to be happy and hip we need to have certain things.

The last time I checked Amazon.com for titles containing the phrase "having it all," more than 133,000 listings came up. Obviously, we are still trying to figure that one out.

Growing up in the 60s and 70s, I was indoctrinated with the belief that I could have it all. I rarely challenged this belief. Only when I was in extreme physical pain or emotional suffering would I even wonder if I was on the wrong track.

The truth is that we *can* have it all. The creative spark of life that is infinite intelligence is limitless. We can have it all, just not all at the same time. But nobody told us that. Many women have knocked themselves out trying. We got distracted. We forgot what's important. Our priorities have shifted. We got lost in the shuffle. These women have worked hard for what they've got. Many women have managed to get everything they needed and wanted, at least occasionally. Yet many continue to feel dissatisfied.

As a society of die-hard consumers we work hard at accumulation. Shopping has become a recreational sport, and some of us have become Olympic contenders. I blame it on our hunter-and-gatherer genes. "Give me more, for less," we demand as we park our cars on lots that were once home to plants, animals and picturesque landscapes. In the free world, anyone can have almost anything, if they have the money. Regardless of your age, social status, education or cultural background, if you have the money you can buy the next must-have item that will give you the next buzz.

According to the *Wall Street Journal*, recent research has identified that buzz as dopamine, the brain chemical responsible for feelings of pleasure and well-being. Research suggests that even window shopping releases dopamine into the brain. This chemical is associated with addictive behaviors and drug use. Did you ever wonder where the saying "If all else fails, go shopping," comes from? Popular thought would have us believe that shopping will suffice as a panacea for all our problems.

Our culture of consumption would have us believe that when we "have" certain things, we can "do" more of what we want, and then we will finally "be" happy. We are off on a wild goose chase, working to *have* more so that we can *do* what we need to do to *be* happy. Is it any wonder that we feel overwhelmed and experience little peace in our day-to-day lives?

Peace will come when we reverse the process of this road to dissatisfaction. First, we must *be* our truth and acknowledge that we are one with Spirit. Then, by opening our hearts to our spiritual selves in whatever we *do*, we discover we *have* more than we ever thought possible. The key to living a fulfilling life is allowing your destiny to unfold as it should.

I FEEL I HAVE HAD A PRIVILEGED AND BLESSED LIFE. This is not because I have lived in castles or driven fancy cars. Many of my privileges have come when financially, physically, and emotionally I was not on top of my game. Not even close. Some of the greatest gifts I have been given were not of a material nature. That is not to say I don't appreciate the diamond bracelet from a lover, or the rhinestone one from my son. But these gifts are fleeting and temporal; they could get lost or stolen, or the gems could fall out.

Over the years I have learned that connecting with Spirit at a deep level is among the most precious gifts that a person can have. The knowledge that we are loved by an unlimited force beyond our earthly experience cannot be bought. Many people are literally killing themselves trying to "have" that experience. We want to have it all, as though we can go out and buy the experience of peace and happiness within. But some things are priceless.

Once that deep source of love is allowed to permeate your soul, there is no going back. Yes, you can get distracted with other lesser pursuits, but the sweetness of our Creator's love, once tasted, is never forgotten. It doesn't matter how many pairs of shoes you buy, or how many orgasms you can have — these excitements soon pale, and once again you are left with yourself. The glow of the initial excitement is gone once the shoes hurt your feet or become scuffed. The orgasms are soon forgotten when your lover forgets to call as he said he would, or is late for an important engagement. Pseudo-happiness is temporary at best, but it does not light up your eyes and fill your heart with the love that spills over.

Having tasted the sweet nectar of love, the Feminine Heart will never forget the intensity of light that filled her body — the pulsing fullness of life itself, the ecstatic bliss of love. That is happiness. That is pure joy. This is when you exude pure radiance and beauty. The indescribable light that shines out of the eyes of people who have let Spirit into their lives and hearts is the most attractive quality there is.

When we live from the inside out, we don't need approval from the outside world. Instead, we can trust and approve of ourselves. There may be times when we feel as though we are going through life on our own, but with Spirit at our side, we are never alone.

Musings & Blessings

WHAT PART OF HAVING IT ALL ARE YOU MISSING? If your connection with the Creator doesn't satisfy, ask yourself what you need to do to express more love, more often?

Breathe deeply, go inside and ask what message Spirit has for you. The Feminine Heart, once expanded, can never go back to its previous size. After every heart-stretching experience, do you find that your capacity to give love has expanded? Notice the feeling in your heart after you offer your love. Breathe into that feeling, and give thanks for all that life has to offer.

The next time you feel the need to "have" something ask yourself: Do I really need it? How many do I already have? Will it last a long time? How often will I use it? Can I borrow it from a friend instead? Is it recyclable?

The next time you feel compelled to take on "one more thing," ask yourself what would happen if you didn't do anything. By denying yourself the chance to do "nothing," you may be depriving yourself of the chance to do "something" — something that will make a difference in your life, or in the life of someone else.

Breathing in love and light, let go of any tension in your body as you exhale. While in that place of quiet peace, ask yourself, "What do I need now that I have not been given?" Listen for the guidance of the message that comes back. Give thanks. You are loved.

The best effect of fine persons is felt after we have left their presence.
– RALPH WALDO EMERSON –

We Can't Get No Satisfaction

My Darling Feminine Heart:

Thank you for helping me to relax
deeper into myself.
Your clear vision and purpose
allow me such freedom
that I am healed by the radiance
of your love.
Thank you, my darling Goddess,
for helping me to relax.

Many women today feel a sadness we cannot name.
Though we accomplish much of what we set out do to,
we sense that something is missing in our lives
and — fruitlessly — search "out there" for the answers.
What's often wrong is that we are disconnected from an authentic sense of self.
— EMILY HANCOCK *—*

ASK YOURSELF ON A SCALE OF 1 TO 10 HOW SATISFIED YOU ARE. Working with many women over the years as a professional matchmaker and workshop facilitator, I was always surprised at how many women were dissatisfied with their lives. Many women are hard-pressed even to say they are happy — forget about joyful, blissful or ecstatic. The number of women who had difficulty expressing their deepest Feminine Heart came close to 80 per cent.

This number doesn't surprise me. Many of the women I meet today are fatigued and depressed because they have suppressed their feelings, and have no connection to their inner Spirit. Working with women on a deeper level, through workshops and retreats, I discovered that the feminine essence is being pushed underground. In most industrialized countries, where a high level of masculine energy exists, there is a lot of unhappiness and despair amongst many of the most accomplished and successful women that I talk to.

Some women are too tired even to complain about their state of affairs. It is almost as though they have succumbed to their half-hearted existence and do not have the energy to do anything about it. In my travels around the world I have met radiantly happy and contented women, but they are few and far between.

While working as a healer, I noticed a reoccurring theme with many of my female clients. Women would break down in tears on the massage table when I worked deeply on certain areas of their bodies. It wasn't physical pain causing the tears to flow, but the emotional pain they had been holding in their bodies that they were finally willing to release. After several years of experiencing the pain of not communicating and sharing her heart openly, the Feminine Heart does not feel sadness, pain, hurt or betrayal. She cannot feel anything. The Feminine Heart has shut down.

To keep our hearts closed so that we can't feel what is going on in our mind and our bodies, we medicate ourselves with anything that relieves us from our inner feelings – food, shopping, sex or another episode of *Desperate Housewives*. But we can distract ourselves from who we are "being" for only so long. The body finally responds to the deflated Spirit and the discouraged mind. Sadness takes over and lodges itself as physical "dis-ease" in susceptible places throughout our bodies. Physical problems become the last manifestation of a spiritual imbalance.

This is true across all countries, across all cultures, across all income levels and across all levels of success. "Women have higher rates of depression," says Dr. Myrna M. Weissman, epidemiologist and psychiatry professor at Columbia University School of Medicine in New York.

It stands to reason that other developed countries have similar statistics. Probably worse. In March 2004, Health Canada reported that 1 in 10 Canadians is on anti-depressants. Those numbers are from people who report their symptoms. According to a report from the National Institute of Mental Health, many depressed people do not report their symptoms. More people than you know are on some form of Selective Serotonin Reuptake Inhibitor (SSRI). Start doing your homework. How could you help your sister open her heart wider so that she does not have to suffer needlessly?

These depressed women are the automatons of our age, not feeling deeply about anything but existing only on the surface of life. Those women are not the only ones affected by depression. The repercussions of the Feminine suppressing her heart affect everyone in her life — family members, friends and colleagues. Nobody gets to benefit from her healing radiance when her Feminine Heart is closed.

The less we express the innate gifts of our Feminine Hearts, the less light and radiance we have to share with others. The heart is a muscle that must be exercised like any other muscle. From a spiritual perspective, the more you can open the valves to your heart, letting the love flow through you, the more energetically empowered you will feel.

Don't be afraid. Trust in the process. There are times when we need help and assurance but no one is around to help or support us. Or so it would appear.

I have been blessed with loving friendships with several wonderful women and men who have passed on to the other side. When I close my eyes now, I can connect with their Spirits. I feel them with me. I listen to any messages I receive while they are with me. When our hearts are open, there is so much love available to us from unlimited sources.

Musings & Blessings

WHEN YOUR HEART IS OPEN, you attract more of what you want. What is stopping you from experiencing your heart's deepest desires? Do you feel that someone is putting a lid on your ability to fully express the radiant love and joy that is your birthright? Are you giving them permission to do so? Why are you giving them that power? What is the payoff that you are getting from not being the powerful and wise woman that you know yourself to be?
If you're not being an angel of love and light, who are you being?

We are not human beings having a spiritual experience.
We are spiritual beings having a human experience.
— PIERRE TEILHARD DE CHARDIN —

Sick & Tired of Being Sick & Tired

My Darling Feminine Heart:

I haven't forgotten about you
although days pass where I don't stop
to acknowledge and respect your needs.
I know you are there.
When I don't stop to say "hello"
I feel so tired, empty and sad.
Please forgive me
for putting everything ahead of you.
I love you.
I thank Goddess for not allowing me
to forget you; my best friend.

> *Heavy thoughts bring on physical maladies;*
> *when the soul is oppressed, so is the body.*
> – MARTIN LUTHER –

THE FEMININE HEART'S DEEPEST DESIRE is to give and receive love. This is the juice that makes us feel alive and connected to those around us. If only we had more time to focus on what gives us the greatest joy and happiness. Super moms and extraterrestrials excluded, women today are overextended. Physically, emotionally and spiritually, there never seems to be quite enough time and energy to do everything we want.

Genetically, we are programmed to give. That is the nature of the feminine sexual essence. But if we aren't able to receive deeply as well, our circuits get blown out. When we are not in the now, we are out of sync with ourselves, which creates tension in our minds and bodies. This tension accumulates, but we don't usually notice until it manifests physically and we get sick.

We get so tired that we don't even have the energy to fake it. So we check out. We do things to try to fill ourselves up with something, anything — food, clothes, shoes, sex, alcohol or chocolate. You fill in the blank. We feel empty. We are tired to the core. If we could just sit in the blissfulness of the moment, we could get a break from our aching bodies, tired minds and derailed spirits.

Depression, anxiety and unexplained sadness — we can say that these conditions are a normal part of living; that feeling these emotions is normal. But over time, if we continue to let these emotions keep our hearts closed, we will suffer. The number of antidepressants and mood-altering substances given out by the medical establishment shows that many people have shut down to the point where they can no longer experience the joys of life. Without the highs or the lows, we live our lives flat-lining — coasting along, without any real feelings. Automatons of the new millennium, the medicated do not feel deeply about anything. Only the surface exists. The Feminine Heart, however, doesn't do well living on the surface. The surface does not fill her heart, and a heartless woman is a woman who has forgotten her natural gifts.

When we push down our feelings, they come back to haunt us again. By allowing our feelings to come into full expression, we give thanks for the messages that they bring, and then let them go. This is one of the biggest perks of living in the moment. As we let the tide of feelings and emotions wash over us, each new feeling almost immediately replaces the last, keeping us in the present. This is not an easy task, especially if the feeling that swells inside demands our forgiveness. That's where the angels leave the pack. With their big wings, they are able to fly above earthly traumas, and raising their hearts closer to Spirit they find forgiveness, even for the most ruthless of transgressors.

I am in awe of people who have freed themselves from the pain in their heavy hearts by forgiving the people who have harmed their children. These people have the utmost capacity to forgive; they deserve the title "earth angel."

To protect ourselves from being hurt, we slowly shut the door to our hearts. After a while, we don't dare open the door even a crack. But if we leave our heart's door closed too often, or for too long, our vital energy starts to vibrate at a lower frequency. Despair and disease insidiously creep in. When we hit middle age our bodies do not lie to us anymore, and we discover the physiological and psychological ailments that closing our hearts for so long produced.

Not sharing our Feminine Hearts is one thing, but we can actually infect others with our negative thoughts and energy. This is a big step toward spiritual awareness and personal growth. Once we accept responsibility for our feelings and experiences, we embark on a new path of self-discovery and personal empowerment.

We may not know how to go forward in that next step — but we know we must. There is no power in blaming others for our situations or experiences. There is no power in playing the victim.

In *Why People Don't Heal and How They Can*, author Caroline Myss, PhD, shares examples of why people choose to be sick. She explains that people choose to hold on to thoughts and patterns that do not allow them to have their full and radiant health. The experience of being sick gets them things that they want in life that perhaps they never received as a child; things such as attention, concern, and maybe even love. But never does it give them self-fulfillment as radiant beings.

The greatest sense of joy and being alive is when we are deeply and intimately connected with other human beings, giving and receiving love. There are many levels and kinds of intimacy. It is possible to feel intimate with every living thing. The important aspect of intimacy is that we feel, touch or experience *ourselves* deeply. We feel more of who we are.

Musings & Blessings

WHEN WAS THE LAST TIME YOU FELT incredibly alive and vital? Do you have the energy to do things that are important to you on a daily basis? I don't suggest that you should try conquering the world, but rather that you have the vitality to share the best of what you have to offer.

If you are lacking vitality, what are you doing that is not serving your heart's desire? If you are sick, look at the thoughts and beliefs that you are hanging on to. Are they life-supporting, or are they sucking you dry?

When we are truly expressing who we are in every moment, there can be nothing but pure love — which, for the Feminine Heart, is the vitality of life.

Worry is like a rocking chair — it keeps you moving but doesn't get you anywhere.
– CORRIE TEN BOOM –

When the Student is Ready

My Darling Feminine Heart:

When we met
I had no idea what lessons
we were to teach each other.
When we departed
our footprints remained imprinted forever
on each other's souls.
Thank you, Goddess,
for guiding those who teach me
what I need to learn.

When the pupil is ready, the teacher will appear.
– a ZEN saying –

I HEARD ONCE THAT PEOPLE COME INTO OUR LIVES FOR A REASON, a season or a lifetime. When we first meet someone, we don't understand why our Creator has placed that person before us. This is one of the most important reasons why we need to show loving kindness to everyone we meet. Let the light of your pure heart shine, so there are no mistakes.

People come in and out of our lives all the time. In the matchmaking profession, we would match potential partners on their values. The most important considerations were how people liked to spend time, how they liked to spend money, and the kinds of people with whom they liked to associate. I saw how quickly people would eliminate the possibility of meeting someone who matched or complemented their values because their potential partners didn't meet some other, less-important criterion. I heard all the reasons why people would exclude meeting someone who I felt would offer an opportunity for a workable relationship. "They don't have enough hair, they have too much hair, they are too old, they aren't old enough, they don't have children, they have too many children," and the list went on and on. Rarely did my clients stop to think about what they could learn from — or what they could teach — the other person.

If we are too quick to judge, we often miss the gift that person may be offering us. Because we are all one Spirit, we are always the student and the teacher. We can learn from the youngest innocent child, as well as from the oldest well-lived person. We also have much to teach others with our wisdom, our experience, our pain and our love.

Relationships are symbiotic — the teacher and the student are there to embrace the energy that exists between them, so that both are gifted by the presence of the other. Without a student, there is no teacher. Without a teacher, the opportunity for the student does not exist.

Musings & Blessings

BE AWARE OF THE PEOPLE WHO PASS through your days and your life. What do they have to teach you? How open are you to learn from them? Are you holding back from sharing yourself in ways that could contribute to someone's learning and growing? Are you being stingy with your knowledge and energy? Do you know that you have something to offer, but find yourself holding back because of the fear that it may not be accepted? Or are you just being apathetic?

Let your light shine, girl — you will be teaching that love exists in the hearts of many. This is one of the greatest gifts you can give. When your heart is open, you are always available to learn about the wonders of life, and about the capacity of your own heart to give and receive love.

What else do you really need to know?

It is one of the most beautiful compensations of life that no man
can sincerely try to help another without helping himself.
– RALPH WALDO EMERSON –

Living Consciously

My Darling Feminine Heart:

When I play small
no one sees me
and I don't have to live full out.
I can hide and whine
but nothing good
comes out of it.
Yet, when I work with you
together
the work is made light…
and we laugh and dance.
We have more power
when we co-create with another.
Thank you, Goddess, for co-creating with me.

How you do anything, is how you do everything.
— T. HARV EKER —

MANY PEOPLE SPEND THEIR LIVES NOT THINKING about how much they can put into life, and what they will get out of it. With an average lifespan of 75 years, most people spend 6 to 10 hours a day sleeping. That takes up about one-third of their lives, or 25 years spent in a state of unconsciousness (some people spend a good portion of that time fretting about not sleeping, as in our stress-filled world more and more people are experiencing insomnia).

That leaves us with about 50 years. Another 10 years or so are spent in the pursuit of pleasure, entertainment, or gossiping about others, which leaves us

40 years or so for eating, family responsibilities, work, taking care of our bodies and maintaining our worldly possessions. When we get through all this, we barely have time for anything else.

The days pass quickly as we run from one activity to the next, barely stopping to enjoy a meal in the company of those we love. What are we so busy running to and from?

The light workers of this world are aware of the earth's imminent demise, and are consciously using their time and energy to create more love and light on the planet. They are educating themselves and others to promote planetary peace, and to dissolve the darkness and destruction so prevalent today.

OUR BODIES ARE COMPOSED OF TRILLIONS OF CELLS; each holding the possibility of Spirit's infinite intelligence. This intelligence is not something that can be found in the classrooms of our educational systems, but rather it is the knowledge that is gained from going inside, and from concentrating on the guidance within.

When our hearts and minds are in a receptive mode, free from distractions and the business of lesser pursuits, we have the wisdom of the ages available to us. When our mind is in this receptive mode, we can bring in the data to solve our business and personal problems.

Every person is a representative of the infinite, and we can utilize that power in everything we do. When you want to manifest or produce something, do not rely only on external sources. Go deep inside and seek the infinite source of wisdom. All ideas, inspirational thoughts and writings, vibrations of music and inventions are already recorded in the annals of our Creator. There you will find everything you need in the pursuit of your endeavor.

By increasing the receptivity of your intuition, you will have everything you need to accomplish that which your heart most desires. Calmness of thought and action, along with the condensation of experience, will assist this receptivity and allow you to access infinite wisdom. Do not do things haphazardly, but do the things that are most important first, with heartfelt enthusiasm and attention.

It is easy to get caught up in myriad distractions that make up our world of so-called entertainment. Rather than spending time watching the latest soap opera or "reality" television show, create your own life story — one with meaning, purpose and passion. As the writer, creator and director of the conscious life that you have chosen, you will never have to complain about your story having a bad ending.

Musings & Blessings

How do you consciously create the outcome of your hours, days and years? Are the days slipping by without letting you realize the dreams and aspirations you have for yourself, for your loved ones, and for the planet at large?

Do you find yourself drawn to people, ideas and things that you know not only bring down your vibratory rate, but actually cause you or others harm? What kinds of movies, books, computer games and television shows are you spending your precious and limited time on?

Our lives on this planet are short. We can choose to consciously use whatever time we are given to express more of who we are, rather than react to our surroundings or the pervasive cultural norm. We can be leaders, consciously shedding our light wherever we go, or followers of unenlightened thoughts and ideas. At this time in the planet's evolution, do you feel you have a choice? What do you choose?

Breathe in clarity of thought. Breathe in love.

I cry and shed tears when clouds gather round my heart,
and when the light of my soul is covered from my sight.
– Hazrat Inayat Khan –

Part Two

Deep Purpose

Sharing the Gifts from the Feminine Heart

My Darling Feminine Heart:

I know that I have so much to give.
My heart aches when I am not living
the truth of who I came here to be.
When days evaporate into years and
my deepest gifts remain unopened in my heart
the longing shows up in my face …
 a dried-up riverbed that once nourished the life
along its banks.
But then I remember
my purpose is to give my love fully.
In that moment my joy returns.
Once again my love is flowing.
Thank you sweet Spirit for reminding me
of my deepest purpose.

If I could choose one great gift that the world is neglecting
I would choose feminine energy. It is what we need to save the world.
– MACRINA WEIDERHEHR, MD –

I N MY WORK AS A CAREER COUNSELOR AND PROFESSIONAL MATCHMAKER, many people tell me the same thing. They know they have some unique talent but they just haven't discovered it, or they don't know how to express it. It may have nothing to do with what they do at work, or how they earn a living. What they know, though, is that they have some special gift to contribute.

At an early age we are not confused by this. It is natural. Young girls display an innate knowledge of the feminine gift of giving and receiving love. Watching a two-year-old nurture her sick baby doll seems so natural. It also seems natural when she plays dress-up by putting a flower in her hair, knowing that the natural beauty of the flower enhances her own beauty, and asks, "Do I look pretty?"

As she grows and develops, her feminine gift will continue to grow with her. Over time, however, if this gift is not acknowledged and rewarded she will leave it behind like a once-treasured Christmas present that has lost its magic. Sometimes she will solemnly place this forgotten gift in a dark corner of the closet of her mind. Then, perhaps, one day she will stumble across it again. When that happens, she has a choice. She can take her feminine gift of love out of the closet, dust it off, and share with others. Or she can leave it untouched, until finally one day it gets tossed into the garbage heap, unused and wasted.

To help reconnect with those aspects of ourselves that we have forgotten, in my workshops and presentations we practice giving and receiving this gift of love. This book is a gentle reminder that our feminine gifts can be renewed and shared.

We can give several gifts at once. The Feminine Heart can multi-task with ease. For example, when visiting a sick friend you may bring some creatively prepared and beautifully presented food. Perhaps you fill a vase with fresh flowers and set it by her bedside, then rub her back, soothing her sore, bedridden muscles. Then, intuitively, you share a private little joke that makes her laugh with spontaneous delight, helping her heal as she forgets her pain and suffering.

In this scenario, you are sharing the gifts of compassion, nurturing, beauty, healing, intuition and love. Your friend won't be sick much longer — she will be healed by the radiance of your love and light.

In this section, I present a list of God-given feminine gifts. My intention is not to give you more things to do. I know you already have way too much on your plate. I give you this list hoping that you will use it to find ways to be more of who you came to be. However you spend your life, my prayer is that you do it with your heart wide open.

Although the following 28 feminine gifts are listed in alphabetical order, they are all at different times, equally important and valuable. When given in love with an open heart, the receivers of these gifts will be blessed by your radiant feminine energy. The receivers, in turn, will have that much more to give others, because these gifts are limitless. These gifts keep on giving.

Musings & Blessings

WHAT THINGS DO YOU DO THAT ARE "JUST YOU?" Do you see these things within yourself? Perhaps you offer these things so naturally that you don't recognize them as gifts. What aspects of yourself would you like to express more of? Make a conscious effort to share those pieces until they become a natural part of your repertoire.

Start small, but with awareness. Even the smallest gift can make a big difference in the life of someone who is hurting, lonely or sad. Never feel that giving your gifts won't make a difference, because each act of giving sends a message that there is an abundance of love in the universe.

You are love, and you share that with others by offering your feminine gifts. Be generous. Remember, love begets love.

There are only two ways to live your life. One is as though nothing is a miracle. The other is as though everything is a miracle."

– ALBERT EINSTEIN –

The Gift of Abundant Love

My Darling Feminine Heart:

There are times
When I must go deep
to find that place of love.
But when I do
I'm always assured
that the well never runs dry.
The more love I offer
the more love comes back
in myriad wonderful
and mysterious ways.
Thank you, Goddess,
For showing me who I am…
a never-ending fountain
of love.

In the opening to the abundance of the universe, anything is possible.
— MELISSA HARRIS —

EVERYONE ON THIS PLANET NEEDS LOVE. I have yet to have a client, friend or member of my family tell me, "You know, I just can't take it anymore! I'm getting too much love in my life."

If you happen to defy the odds, I congratulate you. You are plugged directly into the socket of the divine Spirit that exists everywhere. Let your light shine brightly, and keep it glowing. The rest of us must practice. It is only through our awareness of self and the practice of love that we become proficient at giving and receiving love.

Throughout time, humans have tried to capture the subject of love — in written words, in sweet songs from the heart, and in plays and movies. Love is the universal life force inherent in everything we yearn to experience. As children of our Creator, our destiny is to express that aspect of life that is love. We spend a great deal of our short time on this planet trying desperately to get more love. Yet when we are truly open to love, we know there is no limit to the love that we are.

As enlightened women, we know that we have the power to open up and connect with the divine faucet of love. We are always given a choice in how we respond to life's situations. We can turn the faucets of our hearts wide open, letting the love come gushing out and spraying everything in its path, or we can choose to open the faucet just enough to let a little love dribble out, sharing and nurturing only a fortunate, favored few. Or we can just leave the faucet closed and attempt to deal with the back-swell of pressure caused by love longing to break free.

There is no limit to love. We do not need to be conservationists. In fact, quite the opposite. When we do not use and share the love within us, we actually start to implode. We intuitively know that love is our natural birthright, and by not sharing it we work against our true nature. When we consciously share all the love we have to offer, we begin undoing the negativity that exists as the result of fear.

I call it love bombing. Heaven knows that there is enough violence on this planet. Let us be feminine spiritual warriors by shedding light, by bombing others with love instead of with artillery or with messages of hate, jealousy and fear.

The Feminine Heart needs to share and nurture, as well as to receive love. When we give our love away, it comes back to us. There is no shortage of target audiences. See where your heart feels the most expanded — try kids, animals, plants, men, women, the elderly. The sky is the limit. Everything is held together by love. That is the juice of life. There can never be too much love on this planet. The more you give love, the more you feel. It is limitless.

Nevertheless, you don't have to look far to see how much of our world is ruled by fear. Many contemporary thinkers have been influenced by *A Course in Miracles* by the California-based Foundation for Inner Peace. These thinkers share within their messages the principles of love and fear. If you are not operating from a place of love, fear is behind the thought or action that you are experiencing. Marianne Williamson is one of my favorite teachers on the information contained in *A Course in Miracles*. I have read many of her books and have enjoyed listening to her speak on several occasions. Her speeches are similar to those of other people whose ideas resonate with the changes in humanity as we become more conscious. Like Marianne, many other people on our planet are evolving in their thinking at a rapid pace. At some point in our lives we've all been hurt and had our hearts trampled on, but some people have decided not to let it ruin their lives. By seeing their part in the whole drama, they are willing to forgive. In forgiveness, they are helping to heal our planet.

Musings & Blessings

DO YOU FIND YOURSELF LIMITING THE LOVE YOU ARE GIVING, as though there is only so much to go around? Do you save it for those special people in your life, or are you willing to risk sharing your love with everyone?

Whenever you feel down or heavy-hearted, try giving away more of your love. There is no better medicine than love. When you give it away, you heal yourself of the belief that there is a lack of love in your life. When you accept responsibility for being the co-creator of all life, you accept the wisdom of *being* love. You go, girl!

In spiritual terms, to be in love is only natural.
It is our departure from love that is unnatural.
— DEEPAK CHOPRA —

The Gift of Adaptability

My Darling Feminine Heart:

I will be the consummate professional
when I start my new job tomorrow.
I just need to be a mother to my children before I leave
and a sex Goddess to my husband tonight.
In the time between, I will wear the many hats
of caterer, seamstress, tutor and therapist to a dying friend.
No problem — I will be ready for work tomorrow.
Thank you, Goddess, for my gift of adaptability.

A woman's life can really be a succession of lives,
each revolving around some emotionally compelling situation or challenge,
and each marked off by some intense experience.
– WALLIS SIMPSON, Duchess of Windsor –

THE GIFT OF ADAPTABILITY IS SO MUCH A PART OF BEING A WOMAN that I hadn't even included it in my list of 28 feminine gifts. My dear friend Dr. David Chu, a respected holistic healer and acupuncturist, pointed out that this gift was missing from my list. I had taken it for granted.

Women throughout the ages have been accused of being changeable and capricious, yet when accompanied by wisdom this is a strength. Depending on our stage in life — maiden, mother, wise woman — our adaptability will be affected by our level of experience and wisdom. Throughout our lives our bodies, minds and spirits are continuously adapting. As our feminine bodies grow and develop our hormones change, and our bodies adapt. Our emotions are affected as well.

Throughout our fertile period of life, every month we journey through our feminine cycle adapting to the ebb and flow of our hormones. Approximately every 28 days our bodies prepare to accept new life, but when it is not host to healthy sperm, the cycle continues yet again.

When women become pregnant, physically and emotionally our bodies once again undergo a huge adaptation in bringing a new life into the world. Three months after conception, our sleep patterns begin to change as our bodily functions adapt to the life inside us. We find ourselves waking up in the middle of the night, our bodies preparing for months in the future when we must wake up to feed our hungry and crying infants.

Although many men today have become much more involved in the nurturing and raising of children, their lives are not altered in the same way as the lives of women. A few days after the birth of my son, I remember my former husband was back at his job, having lunch with the guys and carrying on as before our child was born. I adapted to a completely new routine. Having given up my career I now was alone at home, cut off from my colleagues, completely focused on the care and well-being of my new infant.

Perhaps that is why most women live longer than men. Our innate gift of adaptability allows us to move and flow through life more easily than men. Our feminine essence is able to flow freely. Our energy moves quickly and intuitively to the situation at hand, with less struggle and tension. This God-given gift of adaptability helps us respond quickly, serving others where our energies are most needed, whether at home, in the community or in the office.

Musings & Blessings

HOW HAS THE GIFT OF ADAPTABILITY SERVED YOU THROUGHOUT YOUR LIFE? When you find yourself being inflexible, how does it make you feel?

When do you find yourself most frustrated? Is it usually when you have to juggle several balls in the air at once? Although the Feminine Heart is graced with the gift of adaptability, it is important to offer this gift with grace. Breathing deeply, and filling your heart with love while juggling, makes it that much more effective and rewarding.

If you are counseling a friend on the phone while stirring a burning pot and watching your toddler climb onto the kitchen counter — breathe in love, and give thanks that you are so capable and adaptable. Don't forget to exhale any tension that you are holding in your body. Better yet, give yourself time to be alone with your Higher Self to recharge your batteries, so that your light will burn to its maximum radiance.

True life is lived when tiny changes occur.
– LEO TOLSTOY –

The Gift of Beauty

My Darling Feminine Heart:

When I look into the mirror
I see a form that sometimes
I do not recognize.
Where did these lines and shadows come from?
When I look directly into the eyes
of the woman staring back at me
I see the fair maiden who has never left.
I smile at her.
She smiles back, reflecting all the beauty
of the feminine essence that I am.
I breathe in her sweet fragrance...
that delicate fragrance lingers within me still.
Thank you, Goddess, for the gift of eternal beauty.

She whose soul houses a kind heart is never short on beauty.
– AUTHOR UNKNOWN –

WESTERN CULTURE IS OBSESSED with youthfulness and looking good. Advertising media are constantly selling the message that youth and beauty are the coveted ticket to happiness. Unfortunately, this myth is targeted mainly at women.

Even more unfortunately, the women who have bought in to this myth believe that their self-worth is determined by the latest trends in popular culture. Their focus is on external physical beauty, rather than on internal spiritual radiance.

No matter how beautiful women are, we always compare ourselves to others. This is not a healthy or wise thing to do. Someone is always slimmer, younger or more beautiful. If we have not developed our consciousness beyond the physical plane, we will never feel satisfied with our physical attributes.

The phenomenon of eating disorders, where women are literally starving themselves to death to meet some man-made ideal of what it means to be beautiful, is rampant. We have forgotten about our own God-given beauty — that unique gift given to each and every woman. It is only recently that the medical community has started seeing the importance of healing the spiritual aspect in women who have eating disorders — disorders that ultimately affect their physical well-being.

With all the hype on youth and beauty, a huge marketing and advertising conspiracy makes us think that we can buy a piece of that dream. And buy we do. Billions of dollars every year are spent on advertising. The feminine craves to be seen; it is a deep need. Marketers know this. They develop advertising campaigns to create the belief that we need their products if we, too, want to be more beautiful. We have bought in to the idea that beauty comes with a price. The woman with the most money wins. But it is only a shallow form of beauty. In the world of matchmaking, even the most basic of men I have worked with knew that a physically beautiful woman with an unkind heart is not an attractive person.

I N ANCIENT CULTURES, women were trained from a young age to offer their feminine beauty as a gift of love to be honored and treasured. Men paid dearly to enjoy the feminine presence of women who fully understood the power of the gifts they had to offer. The ancient Chinese, Hindus and Greeks used cosmetics and perfumes extensively. Dynastic Egyptian women enameled their fingernails and toenails and carried powder, rouge and lipstick when they traveled. Women have always desired to be physically attractive.

In India, only men who had advanced to a certain level of spirituality were allowed to visit with the temple dancers. These women were trained to express their highest feminine essence, and men considered it a gift to be in their healing presence. Japanese culture trained young girls to express their femininity, offering men the opportunity to more fully experience their masculine energy. Even the wives of these men knew that their husbands would somehow be better men after they had been gifted by a geisha. Of course, to be such an offering, the women themselves had to feel that they were divinely gifted.

In Arthur Golden's best-selling book, *Memoirs of a Geisha*, the main character, Sayuri-san, says, "I've been called beautiful more often than I can remember." Geishas *are* considered beautiful, far beyond their physical attributes. These women were taught how to cultivate that ethereal feminine beauty that is a gift to everyone in its presence, even when they were faced with challenges and hardship.

It was understood that true feminine beauty is much more than pleasing physical characteristics. Graceful movements, the sound of the feminine voice, even the sight of a delicate wrist are enough to take the masculine into his awareness of the polarities between a man and a woman. When he is witness to the feminine essence, a man feels more masculine.

"Adversity is like a strong wind. I don't mean just that it holds us back from places we might otherwise go. It also tears away from us all but the things that cannot be torn, so that afterward we see ourselves as we really are, and not merely as we might like to be," says Sayuri-san.

If we look closely at the women around us, we see that the age of the body has little to do with the beauty that is there. It is the state of the mind, and the expression of the soul, that keeps us young and attractive. Some young women already seem old and jaded far beyond their years. They have lost their radiance and zest for life. Their hollow eyes, no matter how prettily made up with the costliest of cosmetics, show nothing but boredom and apathy.

Negative, critical and moody women delight in little more than criticizing others, or gossiping about the lives of people of whom they know little. The spirits of these emaciated women are starving.

Some other women have kept their minds young and their bodies healthy into their 70s and 80s and older. The joy of being alive emanates from every pore of their well-lived skin. With loving hearts and smiling faces, they remain cheerful and vibrant. They always seem to have a good word to share with others, or a genuine smile to offer a stranger.

The enlightened woman has come to understand that real joy and ecstasy come from contact with the source of all life, from her authentic, spiritual self. If you can find and retain that joy, no matter what happens in your life, you will remain calm and centered in a world filled with countless frivolous distractions.

If you want to stay beautifully youthful, make the effort to contact your inner Feminine Heart regularly through prayer, meditation or time alone. Make a conscious effort to smile every time you see the Spirit in others. Remembering to give a sincere smile to friends, family and strangers — no matter how difficult your circumstances — will indeed help you retain your youthfulness. It will also help you keep your health, and a healthy body is a beautiful body.

W HEN I WAS A YOUNG GIRL, I promised myself that I would never have saggy, soft upper arms like my grandmother. Even in her 50s she had these soft sacks of skin that flapped as she busied herself in the kitchen, or pulled tenacious weeds out of her huge garden. Now, as I watch my body aging, I see my own wings beginning to emerge. I have always been active and athletic, but now gravity is starting to win. My arms are in the early stages of developing wings. I have tried to slow down the process with occasional pushups and lifting weights, but the wings are winning.

In my 40s the wings started budding, poking their heads out of places that once held triceps. My early 40s were filled with the last vestiges of being on "the summer side of life," as once sung by Gordon Lightfoot, a Canadian singer and songwriter. I could no longer fool myself. Time was visibly flowing by, but the tradeoff was that I began to recognize that I am powerful in my wisdom. I started to become comfortable in my own skin.

Now, in my early 50s, I think to myself, "Hey, I earned these wings. These are my wings of honor. Do you know the blood, sweat and tears I had to go through to get these wings?"

This is the trade-off. For the enlightened woman who has nurtured her Spirit as well as her body, the gifts of wisdom and grace are now hers, in place of youth and beauty. Wear those radiant wings with pride and joy, and use them to spread your love. Instead of seeing the soft folds of tissue as the enemy, surrender to the gifts that come along with them.

Next time you notice the arms of a woman, remember that she is so much more than her body. If she is an enlightened woman, she has cultivated her mind and her Spirit, and these newly forming wings are testament to her growing wisdom and consciousness. If she has focused on developing all aspects of her life, and not just her body and physical attributes, the wisdom she has gained makes her more angelic and closer to God. Her wings of wisdom are nothing more than a sign that she has spent many years on this good earth, and that she is starting to prepare to fly home to her Creator. Honor her and cherish her, as there is a good chance that she is indeed an earth angel.

As we go through the stages of life, outward beauty changes. Learn to see these changes as gifts. As our bodies change with the passage of time, we gain more wisdom. There is great beauty in a wise woman. Don't hide your beauty from the world. It is a blessing to all those who catch a glimpse.

THE BEAUTY MEGA-INDUSTRY IS WORTH BILLIONS. If marketers can hypnotize us into believing that our standards and ideals of beauty are consistent with the products that they are selling, we are doomed to unhappiness and, consequently, unattractiveness. If we are always yearning for the next fix that we think will make us beautiful, we will be no more than marionettes being dragged through a man-made stage. No matter how beautifully dressed and costumed the marionette, the cold and lifeless eyes hold no light or love.

Inner beauty is priceless. It cannot be bought. It is something that you are, not something you can buy. Strive to become more Goddess-like, rather than like a lifeless doll. If you want to develop your inner beauty, associate with women whose feminine Spirits reflect wisdom. Often mature women have had enough worldly experiences to know the importance of a beautiful inner life as a means of expressing outward beauty.

Find a mentor in this area of your life. Choose your mentor not for what this woman looks like, for her position in society, or for what she has. More importantly, notice the effect that she has on others. People are drawn to this woman because she has an inner divine attractiveness. No matter how many wrinkles frame their brilliance, her wise eyes emit the light that is the expression of love.

When a woman acknowledges the divine gifts that she brings to the world as an expression of love, she can see the travesty of not sharing those gifts. Spend time developing peaceful, calm and divinely loving eyes by cultivating a loving and open heart. This practice alone can assist in the development of an inner attractiveness that transcends all limitations of physical appearance.

We all know what we have to do to take care of our physical bodies. If, however, we want to be more beautiful every day, we must spend time on the things that contribute to our inner beauty. A healthy body, an enlightened mind, and a loving Spirit all contribute to radiant beauty. The following are simple practices to enhance your God-given beauty. They are the basic principles of good health, which is the essence of radiant beauty.

• Breathe in love and light deeply. Exhale all your impure thoughts and anything that doesn't look like love. This can be part of your daily meditation, or it can become your practice as you go about your daily business. Proper breathing is one of the most important things you can do to radiate more beautifully.

• Drink lots of pure, clean water. Water helps to purify and cleanse the body. When the body is clean, it is easier for the mind to be clean as well.

• Choose healthy food as part of your diet. Every time you make a healthy food choice, you are sending this message to yourself, "I value and love you." If you are not educated in what constitutes healthy food choices, make it a priority to learn.

• Participate in one activity every day that nurtures your soul, and do that just for you. It could be something as simple as taking a long bath, or reading for 20 minutes after dinner. This practice programs your body and your mind to think that you are worth it. This sends a strong message to your psyche, and to others around you. If you think you are worth it, others will too.

• Look in the mirror, breathe, and go inward. Look at yourself. Just look, without judging. Then, going deep inside and accessing that place of eternal knowing, say out loud, "The beauty I see in you is — ." Fill in the blank with something that you sincerely feel and know about yourself. It may be the color of your eyes, or the gentle way you deal with children. Focus more on your inner qualities than on your physical attributes. This is your eternal beauty, and that does not change with time. You may want to repeat the same thing several times, until it resonates in your soul. Or you can choose to acknowledge a different quality every time. Breathe, have fun with it, and honor yourself.

• Learn to smile sincere smiles, no matter how difficult your life seems to be. Nothing is more beautiful than a genuine smile that says, "I honor the beauty and the divinity that resides in you." A smile is one of the highest forms of acknowledgment that we can bestow on one another. Learn to give genuine smiles to all, to family, friends and strangers. One of the secrets to youthfulness is a contagious smile that wells up from your deep inner heart.

• Show kindness and caring to others by offering your assistance. Practice universal love, not just saving it for special friends or family members. Forgive your enemies. Releasing your heart from the constrictions of jealousy or anger makes more space available to fill with love.

• Teach others to see the beauty in themselves. That is the greatest gift you can give a child. Sharing this one thought alone can make a huge difference to the future of our planet.

Musings & Blessings

DO YOU FIND YOURSELF JUDGING THE BEAUTY in others or in things? "She is beautiful, or not." "That thing is beautiful, or not." "I look beautiful, or not." Pay attention to your thoughts, and learn to see the beauty that is everywhere. The more you focus on beauty, the more beauty you will see in and around you.

When we take the time to look, we can see that everything created on this planet has its own unique beauty. Perhaps it doesn't possess the beauty of a rose, but rather the delightful beauty of spring's first dandelion. Remember the words of that old Ray Stevens song, "Everything is beautiful, in its own way." So are you, and you always will be.

You are a wildly beautiful flower. Open the tender petals of your heart and share the beauty of your radiance always. Blossom open to your fullness. Your gift of beauty is invaluable at every stage of life.

Age is something that doesn't matter, unless you are a cheese.
— BILLIE BURKE —

The Gift of Communication

My Darling Feminine Heart:

Sometimes your messages
are so loud they give me a headache.
Could you talk a little softer?
I know I have not been listening
and I am ready to hear you now.
It is only when I am in the moment
with you
that I hear anything you are saying.
When we communicate deeply
I hear my truth
in your loving messages
and you hear the truth in mine.
You and I become one.
Thank you, Goddess, for the gift of communication.

> *To use the same words is not a sufficient guarantee of understanding;*
> *one must use the same words for the same genus of inward experience;*
> *ultimately one must have one's experiences in common.*
> — FRIEDRICH NIETZSCHE —

WOMEN ARE BORN COMMUNICATORS. From the time of conception we communicate with the life within until we pass on once again — even if we don't talk to each other.

The Feminine Heart's ability to communicate goes far beyond the spoken word which research shows accounts for a limited part of the communicated message. Obviously, words aren't the only way to send and receive messages. We learn more when we are communicating with our hearts.

Your Feminine Heart is in direct communion with the divine love of Spirit. When you say a heartfelt "I love you," it is not you who loves, but rather the message of Spirit comes through your words; this is the message that is felt and received by another. It is our state of *being* that is communicated through our words, not what we are *doing* or *saying*.

When we communicate with our hearts, it is not that we check out of the brain altogether, but it is the *intention* of our communication that affects the heart's message. Is the intention of your communication to help, or to hurt? This question is not easy. It requires honesty and awareness. Fortunately, the enlightened woman is willing to do her homework, as she knows she will reap what she sows.

If you want honesty and deep connection in your communication with others, you have to express yourself in that manner. If your intentions are antagonistic, don't expect to attract loving messages. We attract who we are in our innermost hearts.

Today we don't have time for a lot of one-on-one except with our computers, employers and service people as we run our daily errands. We think that when we get home and see the people we love, then we can share our hearts. Wrong! If we wait to share with our families and loved ones, we are wasting precious time.

Most people spend a large portion of their days with people they don't love, let alone like. The average workplace isn't exactly a place of comfort and joy for most employees. But if we spend most of our waking hours with people we don't love, we aren't giving or receiving love. Then, when we get home, if we go to bed with our capacity to love unexpressed, we suffer.

We must communicate love as an intention of life. Not as a part-time hobby, but as a way of living. This is our job. Communicating to others in a way that allows them to see the love that they are is the biggest gift we can give anybody.

When you speak from your deepest heart, your truth, magic happens. Any resistance of the mind is overcome by love and something inside you transforms. This is the power that can open another heart, and the place where miracles can occur. I have made it my mission, to "train minds to start with heart." May I invite you to join with me in that mission? Together we can create a world where love is communicated honestly and freely as a gift to one another.

Musings & Blessings

NOTICE THE INTENTION BEHIND YOUR COMMUNICATIONS. Is the intent to share more love and further open the heart of the person with whom you are speaking? If not, what is your intention? Be honest with yourself.

Awareness is everything. If you are not honest in your communication with yourself, don't expect any better treatment with others. If you want others to be honest and heartfelt with you, you must be that too.

The words you habitually choose also affect how you communicate
with yourself and therefore what you experience.
– ANTHONY ROBBINS –

The Gift of Compassion

My Darling Feminine Heart:

When I see the pain
etched upon your face
a scar
is left upon my heart.
When I hear your sighs
as you give up in despair
my heart sighs too.
When I keep my heart open
I feel the joy and sorrows
contained within your heart …
because our hearts are one.
Thank you, Goddess,
for the tender gift of compassion.

It's not how much we give, but how much love
we put in the doing — that's compassion in action.
— MOTHER TERESA —

THE LATE MOTHER TERESA WAS THE QUEEN OF COMPASSION. This amazing woman devoted her life to service to others. She founded the Missionaries of Charity, a worldwide mission whose members were in service to the poorest of the poor. Her attitude regarding compassion was simple: "We can't all do great things. But we can all do small things with great love."

We can't all be like Mother Teresa. It's unfortunate that there are not more pure-hearted women for today's young women to emulate. If the media focused less on who the starlet of the week is sleeping with, or what she was — or wasn't — wearing at the latest star-studded event, perhaps our young women could focus on where they can make their own newsworthy events by making a positive difference in the world of others.

THE FEMININE HEART ACHES FOR THE ILLS OF THE WORLD. After she has a child of her own, that pain becomes unbearable at times. After the birth of my son, I remember how the suffering of all children affected me at a much deeper level.

In countries where peace is still a relative possibility, our hearts cry out in compassion when in newspapers or on television we see the suffering in war-torn, poverty-stricken countries. Millions of women and children worldwide face blatant suffering as an everyday occurrence — their lives are a series of horrific events.

We are the fortunate few. Perhaps we send money to the disadvantaged or fill gift boxes at Christmas to be sent to impoverished countries. Closer to home, our compassionate hearts can extend kindness in many ways. We give away unused clothing or household articles to charity, we help out the local soup kitchen, or we drop coins in the hats of homeless street buskers.

We are also joining together to form powerful women-led organizations working to serve the needs of the world's most vulnerable. MADRE, the international Women's Human Rights organization based in New York City, has sister organizations worldwide. MADRE is active in places like Iraq and Haiti, where basic survival for women and their families is a daily concern. MADRE's founders understood that women, as the compassionate caretakers of our planet, have a powerful stage upon which to build lasting political partnerships in different communities and different cultures.

"Women in Black," another group of women gathering around the world, honors the lives lost to violence. Started in 1988 by Palestinian and Israeli women uniting to reduce the violence in the Middle East, it has now expanded to include women all over the world.

Even if you don't choose to align yourself with organized groups, there are endless ways to share your compassionate Feminine Heart in your daily world. A Buddhist practice of generous compassion called *metta* involves silently repeating phrases of well-wishing, over and over. Send these wishes to yourself, to your loved ones, to strangers and especially to people living in fear, who need it the most. It costs nothing, takes little time, expands the capacity of the heart and helps in healing the planet.

Musings & Blessings

COMPASSION TUGS ON THE FEMININE HEART ALL DAY LONG. From hearing the whimpers of your new puppy to seeing the devastating photo on the front page of the daily newspaper; our compassionate hearts are constantly being pulled.

Do you open your heart even further when faced with antagonisms? When you feel your heart closing, breathe deeply into your lungs and as you exhale, release the tightening around your chest. Continue breathing until you can feel your heart once again. Act from that place of service, and your compassion will be given back to you.

No one is useless in the world who lightens the burden of it to anyone else.
— CHARLES DICKENS —

The Gift of Creativity

My Darling Feminine Heart:

With you
I co-create my reality.
With you, I manifest
my deepest thoughts and desires.
With you
I create more love in the world.
With you,
I express more of me.
Thank you, Goddess, for expressing yourself
throughout my thoughts, words and actions.

It's time for me to start being Me.
– DIANA, Princess of Wales –

T HE CREATIVE SPARK OF LIFE, the essence of God, is in everything. At its core, feminine essence reflects that divinity. Whether we give birth to a child or birth to a thought, we are continuously creating, evolving and dying. Throughout this process, the gift of creativity permeates every action and thought.

Many people think that creative thinking is a special gift that only a few people possess, but the enlightened woman knows that all her thoughts are creative. She is continuously co-creating with Spirit. There is no separation. We are one.

Many ways exist to increase the creative power of our brains. Some of these techniques may help to release emotional residue from the past, residue that still affects our bodies. Find the technique that works best for you, and use it.

Focus on how you can become free of unresolved emotions, so your creative mind can be free to access the magic of the creative Spirit.

For the Feminine Heart, creativity comes most easily when we learn to release trapped emotional stress. Experiencing the lightness and joy in sharing our creative potential is well worth the effort expended in creating emotional well-being.

As co-creators of life, we have little choice but to evolve consciously. Barbara Marx Hubbard explains in her book, *Conscious Evolution*, "our labor pains began in 1945 with the explosion of the atomic bombs over Japan. This was a sign that the shift to the next stage of our evolution had begun: We would either evolve in consciousness, or self-destruct our system."

Hubbard sees the atomic bomb as the first of three key events that have been critical for human evolution. The second key was seeing ourselves in a magnificent picture of the earth taken from the moon. The first Earth Day occurred in 1970, one year after the first lunar landing.

> The third crucial event of the 1960s is the awakening of women en masse to a new identity, a new function, a new role in evolution. Suddenly, in one generation we saw that our age-old function of massive reproduction had to stop. We began shifting from the all-consuming and heroic effort of birthing and nurturing 5 or 10 children to the newer effort of finding self-expression and meaningful work — moving from the first two basic human drives for self-preservation toward self-evolution and cocreation. (p. 41–42).

Because we have evolved as a species, we yearn to express ourselves in a new creative ways. The ways that you find most satisfying are as individual as you are. The following list (on page 84) was given to me by my creativity coach, Leo Peters. Try any of these suggestions and see what helps release those creative surges that lie latent within.

The more unique ways the Feminine Heart finds to share her creativity, the more blessed the world will be. There are many ways to do that. People all over the planet are waking up to the power of using their creativity to make a difference in the world.

A friend, Nan Thibert, is a wonderfully gifted artist. As founder of the *Sharing Unicorns Project*, Nan is using the creativity of her art to help heal humanity and

Expressing our Creativity

• Be creative by doing creative things (put on different clothes, or change your hairstyle).

• Get in touch with humor. Read the funnies, listen to comedy or musical comedy. Trade funny stories, and share those embarrassing moments. When you've got humor going on, the endorphins are moving.

• Be constructive. Instead of complaining about a pet peeve, come up with constructive ideas to do it better, or finish it. If you come up with a good idea, act on it immediately.

• Start with the end, and work backwards. Picture the idea, product, service or company, and do whatever it takes to make it happen. What would it look like, smell like, feel like?

• Draw the solution. You don't have to be an artist, just express yourself.

• Change your perspective. How might others see your problem?

• Brainstorm. Find the most creative people you know, and use their synergy to develop ideas. Do not let roadblocks get in the way.

• Create your own think tank. Find a room that is free from distractions. Supply pens and paper, and an idea journal. A round table and comfortable chairs work best.

• Adapt other ideas to your situation. Study the latest journals for new discoveries. How might you incorporate your ideas into existing ideas? Think of new ways to combine them, to come up with a totally new way of thinking about things. Try incorporating the masculine side.

• Never stop learning. Read creative literature, take a seminar, or walk down a street you've never noticed before.

bring in the new era of love. Her amazing murals of unicorns express the healing energy of love. Unicorns symbolize purity and joy, and she sees them as a herald for a new era of humanity.

"The oldest writings about unicorns come from ancient Chinese mythology. It was written that to see a unicorn meant that a new era of goodwill and prosperity was dawning," Nan shared with me. "Looking at these magnificent pieces invites people to take a moment and think of something that makes them happy in the face of their daily circumstances. This generates joy, which is an element of love, helping to heal the planet."

While few of us have the extraordinary creative talent of Leonardo Da Vinci or Picasso, research from the field of cognitive science shows that the ability to generate innovative ideas is a gift that we all possess. The ability to think up a novel, original idea seems daunting at times, but often when we open our minds to the possibility it comes in a flash of inspiration.

Musings & Blessings

How can you use your God-given skills and talents more creatively to make a difference in the world? What subjects keep you really interested? What are some small things that you can incorporate each day that will let you live the more creative life that is inherent in all of us, at all times?

The wider we open our hearts to the light, the more creative healing power is accessible to us. Do not squander it. Do not misuse it. As an enlightened woman, ask for guidance. Ask where you can make your biggest contribution, then go and share your creative gifts... life will become easier and more filled with pleasure and fun.

When you create, you don't have the feeling that you are working.
— Michell Cassou —

The Gift of Emotions

My Darling Feminine Heart:

What do you mean, "Stop crying
because it's making you feel sad and uncomfortable?"
Do you tell a monsoon to lighten its load
and expect it to stop
because you are soaked to the bone?
Surely you jest.
When the sparkling salt diamonds create rivulets down my cheeks
I can see and feel the beauty of my cleansed soul.
After all, I am a woman
with no lesser a purpose than the monsoon
to cleanse and nurture everything in its path.
Thank you, Goddess, for my feminine gift of emotions.

*Instead of resisting any emotion, the best way to dispel it is to enter it fully,
embrace it and see through your resistance.*
— Deepak Chopra —

WE DO OURSELVES A HUGE DISFAVOR WHEN WE RESIST who we are and what we feel. The natural state of the Feminine Heart is related to the pulse of life. We are an expression of the infinite. Nature changes her colors and her moods continuously, and we are no different. Daily events affect our thoughts and feelings, creating different emotional responses.

Emotions are energy in motion. Treat them as gifts — they are wellsprings of information if you are willing to experience them. Listen to them like messages from God, allowing them to move through you like a wave washing over a pearl in the sand. The key is not to resist, or to rebel against them as if they didn't exist, but to accept them fully without attachment.

I once heard a joke: "Why can angels fly?" The answer is, "Because they take themselves lightly." This made me smile. The enlightened woman doesn't allow her emotions to push her into action, or reaction. Just stop, pay attention, and listen to what your emotions have to say to you. Once it is fully acknowledged, emotional energy is released back into the ocean of life. Give thanks for the messages of these emotions and breathe deeply, opening your heart to the next wave of emotions. This is a stepping stone to living in the moment. Our feelings are our most genuine paths to knowledge when we trust enough to surrender to them. Walk with confidence and grace.

EMOTIONS ARE THE JUICE OF LIFE. They give us distinctions that make us individual and separate, yet united. The Feminine Heart is open to feeling the different emotions quivering as they pass through our lives. All emotions have a purpose — especially the positive ones. Love, joy, and bliss are emotions that heal. These emotions can bless a heart. Other emotions, when expressed negatively, can blister a heart.

People who have a strong masculine essence   *Emotions are the juice of life.*
may have a heated argument with a friend or
lover, then quickly and easily go back to the task at hand. Some women who have a strong feminine essence, however, feel their emotions deeply but have not yet learned to become like luminescent pearls, letting each wave of emotion wash over them while retaining their luster and radiance. Afraid of the immense power behind their emotions, they automatically resist them.

The enlightened woman doesn't keep a tight rein on her emotions. She is not fearful of the damage they might do if fully expressed. The Feminine Heart knows that feelings do not go away. They are just submerged, waiting to pop up again when given half a chance.

This has given emotions a bad rap. Continuously blocking our emotions traps them within our bodies and drains our feminine energy. When we refuse to experience the message of our feelings, a discomfort occurs that over time manifests as fatigue, sadness or depression. Because of the intricate connection between our physical, emotional and spiritual bodies, blocking our emotions also blocks the vital life force that is our radiant beauty. This ultimately manifests as rage and bitterness, which hardens our hearts and makes our bodies sick. Rage and bitterness do not foster feminine beauty.

When we ask for strength from Spirit, we can summon up the courage to face even the most intense emotion. After we have fully embraced it, and let go of the reins, we discover that the emotion evaporates. When we no longer try to hold on to our emotions, they no longer have a hold on us. When we refuse to acknowledge our emotions, we keep them alive. As long as they are kept hidden within our hearts, they require energy and attention. Once we embrace our emotions and release them from their place of hiding, we are no longer their captors. They are free to be expressed — and they can no longer have control over us.

Emotions are the bridge that connects the body, mind and spirit to your experience and appreciation of life. When you have a healthy body, clarity of mind and freedom of spirit, you truly have it all. The most important thing you can do to keep the energy of emotion moving through you is to breathe deeply, focusing on bringing love into your heart and exhaling anything that doesn't look and feel like love. Continue several times until you feel calm, centered and cleansed. The wave of emotion has receded, once again leaving behind your glistening Spirit.

The world of emotion is part of the domain of the Feminine Heart. The depth of feeling that we experience is directly linked to the openness of our hearts. Many women have shut down their feelings so as not to experience pain, fear, anger, guilt and myriad other negative emotions. In the process, they have lost the ability to feel their positive emotions. They have lost the ability to feel.

As an enlightened woman, you can embrace all of your emotions without fear. Feel the sensations in your mind and body without becoming attached to the emotion. Let it be. When the wave of emotion rolls over you move with it, letting it enfold you in its arms and gently release you once again on the sandy shores of stillness. You can fight the wave, trying to swing against its power and force, but in the aftermath you will find yourself spent and exhausted.

We always have a choice about whether we react to a situation. When we feel the strength of emotion taking over, breathe and relax into the feeling. Struggling with a wave as it attempts to sweep you away is self-defeating. Going with the flow of the wave of emotion is much less painful, and it will bring you to the other side with grace.

If you are faced with persistent negative emotions, try a simple exercise devised by Dr. Gerald Jampolsky, an immunologist who practices a form of therapy called "Attitudinal Healing." Jampolsky suggests that while you are in bed at night, close your eyes and imagine a big garbage can. Put any negative feelings or thoughts that you've had during the day into it. Don't forget those feelings of guilt or fear. Now close the lid tightly and visualize a huge helium balloon taking the garbage can filled with your negative emotions up into the sky. Watch it become smaller and smaller, until it disappears altogether.

Sweet dreams.

Musings & Blessings

COMMON PHRASES USED TO NEGATE THE EXPERIENCE of our emotions by more masculine types are: "Suck it up, sister," or "Stop acting like a woman," or "Pull yourself together." How do you react when faced with similar comments?

Feel your body when you are withholding emotions. Where do you store that energy? How does this affect your mind and your physical health?

Breathing deeply, feel the emotion fully. Let it pass through like a wild storm on a windy night. Then, as the emotion evaporates, love's light will enter once again like the sun's rays seeping out of the darkest clouds.

The heart has its reasons which reason knows nothing of.
— BLAISE PASCAL —

The Gift of Faith

My Darling Feminine Heart:

As the door to my divine heart closes
the light disappears and I sit in darkness
Patiently faith waits outside,
knocking, knocking, knocking —
Slowly I open the door to my heart
and the light of love floods in.
Once again my heart has opened.
I am offered the relentless hand of faith.
I accept.
Once again I am aligned with my true self.
Thank you, Goddess, for offering your hand.

Faith is an invisible and invincible magnet, and attracts to itself
whatever it fervently desires and calmly and persistently expects.
– RALPH W. TRINE –

WHEN OUR FAITH IS WITH GOD, we can have faith in all of life. The universe is upheld by this truth through the operation of cosmic laws. Truth, the ultimate substance, is linked to everything. It is the essential nature of all life. When the truth is hidden, we are left with delusion. When we lose faith, we become disconnected to our source of life, to Spirit. This is the root cause of all unhappiness and despair.

The easiest way for enlightened women to access the gift of faith is to go inside, to connect with the love that exists in our Feminine Hearts, and to give thanks. Breathing in love and connecting with Spirit opens our hearts.

Love never fails. Faith is always there when we love.

When we try to apprehend the truth we can be fooled if we depend solely on our senses of sight, hearing, taste, smell or touch. The mind doesn't always tell the truth. It will draw conclusions from what the senses perceive, and we know that the senses are extremely limited. All things are composed of God's light. Even your body is nothing but electromagnetic waves. This light cannot always be detected by your physical senses, but on an intuitive level it can be perceived by your open heart. Trust your Higher Self to know the truth, as your eyes grow dim and your hearing fades.

We spend much of our days living in the future — not content with how things are now, but anticipating how they will be after we've made them better. Wanting to improve things is a normal and natural feeling. With awareness, however, we come to have faith that things are perfect in each and every moment for what we need to learn. With that acceptance of life, we can start to relax.

Unfortunately, relaxing is something we don't do very well. In our frantic days of trying to be everything to everyone, if we are just ourselves we fear that we are not enough. We fill our days with activities that keep our minds busy and our bodies moving, but our Spirit is often not acknowledged. When we acknowledge Spirit, our faith returns and we can once again relax.

Musings & Blessings

HAVE YOU EVER LOST YOUR FAITH SO COMPLETELY that you sat in total darkness? When you were ready to surrender your heart and move out of the depths of that darkness, did you notice that there was a light on the other side? God's light lives deep in the crevasses of our hearts. When you are willing to go inside and open the doors to your heart, the light of faith will come flooding back.

When you reconnect with your faith, your Feminine Heart will follow its destiny. Your life will be transformed. Your destiny is to make a big difference on the planet. Not someday, when you have extra time, but now.

Now is all there is.

God does not ask your ability or your inability. He only asks of your availability.
– MARY KAY ASH –

The Gift of Family

My Darling Feminine Heart:

My family is a pillar of strength,
but sometimes it crumbles, decays and moves away.
I mourn the loss of those who share my blood.
Yet I have another family.
The golden thread that binds this family is not blood, but Spirit.
Because Spirit never disappears or dies,
it will always be my family.
Thank you, Goddess, for all my family members.

Call it a clan, call it a network, call it a family.
Whatever you call it, whoever you are, you need one.
— JANE HOWARD —

A HAPPY FAMILY IS ONE OF LIFE'S GREATEST BLESSINGS. The need to belong to a greater entity, where we are loved and accepted for who we are, is paramount to a healthy sense of self and a feeling of safety in the world.

Family is the root of existence. It is what has come before us, and it will continue through our children after we are gone. Even if we have no children of our own we have a family, or clan, in our links to the people who share our world.

Today, many of us do not have the luxury of having family members in close proximity. We live in communities, cities and even countries where none of our other blood family members live. For many people, the nuclear family does not exist. Blended families, single-parent families, gay families and adopted families are the norm. This has created a need for people to invent their own "families."

These families consist of the people we choose to have in our lives, people who support us in the same way that our biological family members would support us. These people may come into our lives from many directions, but we usually feel a kindred connection with them.

If you live away from your family or don't have biological family members close by, you can create your own family. Try joining organizations or visiting places where you can contribute your love. The giving of your time and energy to others will attract like-hearted people into your world. Ask God to bring the people who can be your family to you, and trust who shows up. At first glance, it may not appear to be who you are expecting. Have faith and trust — go to that inner place of knowing with an open heart, and your family will continue to widen.

Many distractions take us away from our home and family. Many of us have jobs, family responsibilities, community involvement and an endless variety of tasks needing to be done. Yet the greatest victory we can have is victory in our own homes. This victory comes when we serve as angels emanating our peaceful energy, feeding the people in our households with its strength.

When that source of strength does not exist in the family, its members have no refuge to help shelter them against the storms of life. When people feel that they are alone in the world, they become self-serving and territorial. This does not lead to a world of people working together to create a peaceful planet. Disorder in our society is a result of disorder in the family. The Feminine Heart is acutely aware of this. Today, it seems, some people want to make some changes to the status quo. This book, and others like it, are helping to usher in the new era of love.

Studies at the Vanier Institute for the Family found that 9 out of 10 Canadians believe the ideal situation in families is for one parent to be at home raising the children. Almost all of the employed mothers polled, and 84 per cent of the employed fathers, would work part-time if they could afford to, so they could be at home with their children.

Research shows that these numbers are not significantly different in other industrialized countries. These statistics have put increasing pressure on governments to lower taxes and give parents more disposable income to achieve their ideals.

We also have to take some personal responsibility in making lifestyle choices. In our consumer-driven society we must make choices about what's more important — having the latest things, or spending time with the people who need and love us.

My son and I live away from my biological family. For the past 10 years we have opened our home, and our hearts, to young people from around the world who come to Canada to learn to speak English. Many of these students have become part of our family. Some who came to stay for three months ended up living with us for more than two years. We continue to stay in touch, as they have become members of our universal family.

Opening up our hearts and homes to these students allowed my son and I to experience the humanity that lives in all of us, no matter what culture we come from. When I started this program through our local college, I saw it as another small source of income, one that allowed me to work out of my home while raising my young son. I was responsible for giving the students the experience of living with a Canadian family. My son and I benefited from knowing the people with whom we shared our home and lives. These benefits far outweighed the couple of hundred dollars that I was left with at the end of every month.

Almost every evening we sit down as a family, starting our meal using the simple Japanese grace *Etadakimasu* which, roughly translated, says, "Bless this food, bless the people who prepared it; bless the people who eat it." This works for me as I do the majority of the cooking and I know that blessing the food makes it special, no matter how simple the fare. Dinner is a time of communal offering. It is a time of sharing. For us it is also a time of connectedness, of having a smaller place to come to in the scope of the outside world. A short grace that can be used to show respect for the earth and her bounty is:

> *Earth that gave us all this food*
> *Sun that made it ripe and good*
> *Dear Sun, dear Earth*
> *We pray that ye*
> *Never shall forgotten be.*

The program coordinator calls me to discuss students that she feels would be a good match for my home and living situation. Each time I asked Spirit to send a student who would be a blessing for all involved, and we have been very fortunate to share our home with some wonderful people. Not that it's been without challenges, but the learning that has come out of those challenges has made us more compassionate to people from other cultures.

If you have a family, nurture it. Make it a priority. If you don't have a family, create a network of people around you. Continue to keep your heart open, giving love where possible and receiving love when it comes your way. The need to belong to a greater community is paramount to our sense of self. It is paramount to our survival.

Whatever your family structure looks like, honor it. Celebrate and give thanks for one of life's greatest blessings. As the heart center of our families, we must ensure that we give the best that we have to offer. Like the force of gravity, our love and nurturing is an anchor ensuring that our family members remain stable and secure.

Parenting is a daunting task at times, even for the most well-adjusted adults who have many support systems to fall back on. I admire people who've raised families and children on their own. Single parenting is one of the most challenging tasks an adult can undertake — yet with the divorce rate fluctuating at more than 50 per cent, many children are being raised in single-parent homes, often by their mothers.

Studies have shown that being a mother with young children creates situations where the lack of social support becomes a risk factor for depression. The results of these studies show that women whose husbands are absent, or nonexistent, are more likely than other women to suffer from depression while raising small children under 10 years old — just what these children don't need.

Often there are economic concerns, as well as the social ramifications of being a single parent, which results in considerable stress and frustration.

I have been a single parent for most of my son's life. There have been challenges for both of us.

Our children need positive role models from both ends of the sexual spectrum to help them identify with their own sexuality. If you are a single parent, surround yourself with friends of the opposite sex who will help be a positive role model for your child.

During my corporate career, I had a boss who came back to work three weeks after the birth of her third child. Her child was short-changed because she feared losing her place on the rungs of the corporate ladder. Lured by the rewards of a lucrative job, she chose to give up bonding with her infant son.

Many women feel forced to make such decisions, either for economic reasons, or for fear of not being seen as serious players within their organizations.

We make choices in our lives that have lasting impacts on our children. We become short-term focused in our thinking. We don't see the implications of our choices over the long haul. Sometimes these choices seem difficult, but by trusting our Feminine Hearts we will always make the right choice. Have faith and follow your heart. A family is a treasure not to be squandered.

Musings & Blessings

WHAT ARE YOU DOING TO CREATE MORE LOVE within the context of your home and family life? What are you doing to open the doors to your family, welcoming others who might not be so blessed? Give thanks for your family, whatever shape or size.

Breathe love in and think of your immediate family and your global family. Exhale deeply, letting go of pain and fear. Breathe in love.

*One of the oldest human needs is having someone to
wonder where you are when you don't come home at night.*
– MARGARET MEAD –

The Gift of Femininity

My Darling Feminine Heart:

Let me grace you with my feminine charms
so that you can more fully experience yourself.
My soft beauty,
my sweet sounds,
my graceful movements,
my sweet smells
are all gifts that only a woman can give.
Through sharing my feminine gifts
I feel that my purpose is realized
and my heart's capacity is stretched
even further than before.
In gratitude and love I give thanks
to my feminine Goddess within.

The valley spirit never dies; it is the woman, primal mother.
Her gateway is the root of heaven and earth.
– Lao Tsu –

FEMININITY HAS GONE THROUGH VARIOUS INCARNATIONS over the centuries. From appearing weak and demure to strong and sexy, the way we express our femininity is as individual as we are.

Katherine Hepburn knew what it meant to be a woman. Grace Kelly, Mother Teresa, Lady Di — they all had the feminine spirit shining brightly in their eyes. We know them as that aspect of the divine feminine. These modern-day icons express that knowing and that gratitude.

More powerful and more compelling is a mature woman who knows herself at her core. Conscious of her wisdom and grace, she knows the worth of her Feminine Heart. Women who offer their femininity hold a tremendous amount of personal power.

Working as a matchmaker, I kept hearing the same things over and over again. Men are attracted to, and interested in having, partners who are feminine women. That may seem like a redundant statement, but often it is not. Women who are constantly in their masculine energy are not feminine, no matter how much lace they are wearing.

Be like the ancient temple dancers. Gift men with your deepest yearning and love as an art form. This "will attract and inspire your man's deepest presence, even when you feel tired or not in the mood," says David Deida in *Dear Lover, A Woman's Guide to Enjoying Love's Deepest Bliss*. "If you practice opening so your body is breathing love's fullness — as if you were on the verge of the most loving orgasm you could imagine — he will notice. Remember, he is not at home in life as fully as you are."

Feminine energy is moving into our lives. If we open our hearts and extend our love inward, and then breathe that love outward onto others, we will bless the world. But we need it all — masculine as well as feminine. Together, the masculine and the feminine make magic. The Feminine Heart is ready to be claimed by all who crave her sweet femininity.

Geisha means art. As portrayed in the movie, *Memoirs of a Geisha*, young women were trained to be courtesans in the art of presentation. Everything in their presentation — hair, makeup, dress — was offered in a way that expressed the highest gift of the Feminine Heart.

The trend in fashion right now is once again the feminine. Cocktail dresses, elegance and feminine details are showing up everywhere, from hair clips that accentuate soft curls to classically feminine jewelry such as pearls and real gems. After years of double football pads competing with the boy's uniforms of the 80s, or the gothic and dead looks of the 1990s, it is soothing for a woman to look feminine. Today we are moving toward a new world order, and the dress of the Goddess is returning. It never really went away, it just went underground for a bit.

Dressing with the intention of expressing our femininity, however, is a conscious choice. It helps us express who we are. For the geisha, dressing was an important aspect of her job. Always impeccably groomed, her elegant clothes never showed much skin but left men desiring to see more.

When you are on your monthly cycle, it is important to make the effort to dress more femininely. Instead of dressing the same way as every other time of the month, notice that during your menstrual cycle you feel more feminine, softer and more vulnerable. Forget about the black pants and jeans for a few days. Put on something pretty and feminine. Consider that silky dress you hardly ever wear, or that long, full skirt that shows your feminine shape and flows around your legs but doesn't restrict your movements while you dance. When you wear a dress, you walk and sit differently. You automatically feel more feminine when you wear things that accentuate your feminine essence.

These small things allow you to shift your energy, and they don't take any extra time — you have to get dressed anyway! But it is amazing how they affect your psyche! Use this time in your cycle to connect with the feminine aspect of yourself, and learn how to access that aspect throughout the rest of the month.

One of the exercises we do at my workshops to access the archetype of the feminine queen is to get dressed up in our finery and put on a tiara and heels. It is impossible to slump around with poor posture while wearing a crown on your head. It forces you to hold your head up high, to use good posture and to express that queenly aspect of the Feminine Heart. Try this at home, then carry that feeling of royalty with you as you shop at the supermarket. You will not only hold yourself differently, it will help you express your femininity with grace, poise, and power.

There are many perils to ignoring our feminine nature. When we don't express our inner nature authentically, over time our bodies start sending signals that we are going down the wrong path. I have heard countless stories of physical and emotional suffering from women who have ignored their yearning to express their feminine essence.

L AURIE WAS A CLASSIC EXAMPLE OF A WOMAN who had lost her health by ignoring her feminine expression. When she first arrived at my workshop, she seemed tough. She was dressed like your average man, in jeans, shirt and boots. Her cropped, boyish hairstyle was neat, and her face showed not a trace of makeup. She had an attractive presence about her, but her eyes looked sad and hollow. She did not say much throughout the workshop until the end, when she stood and asked if she could share her story. I could see that she was bursting to share something important. "Of course," I encouraged her.

"I have been working with the militia for the past 13 years," she told the hushed crowd, many of whom sensed that something major was happening for this woman. "During that time I worked mostly with men, and almost every day I wore the same army uniform as the men. To fit in, I became like one of the guys. I thought I was doing a good job at work. For the last year and a half, though, I started losing feeling in the left side of my body. It started as a tingling sensation, but now I have a lot of pain and I have lost feeling in my left hand."

Her voice trembling with emotion and with tears rolling down her cheeks, she continued. "Today, after going through these exercises and once again embracing my forgotten feminine nature, I actually have sensations in my hand again. I can now see what a disservice I did to myself. I am no longer willing to live my life hiding those parts of me that need to be expressed."

The workshop participants sat quietly, in reverence at her honest sharing. Her tough exterior had softened and her eyes, glistening with tears, showed hope and excitement. I knew that she was on track. She was allowing her feminine Spirit back in. For her, there would be no going back.

This is what makes my work so rewarding — supporting others in expressing their true nature is a blessing for everyone involved. When you live in that place of priceless femininity, you bless yourself as well. Fulfilling your destiny as a woman allows you to relax into your truth. It is a time of comfort and joy, as you offer your highest gifts.

Musings & Blessings

How can you offer your gift of femininity throughout your day, no matter how much "stuff" you have to get done? Remember, it's not the doing that will give you as much satisfaction as who you are being while getting your tasks done. By expressing your innate femininity you will not only feel like more of the woman that you are, but others will respond to you with delight. When you are in alignment with your Higher Self, others will also be more authentically who they are.

Don't compromise yourself. You are all you've got.
— JANIS JOPLIN —

The Gift of Girlfriends

My Darling Feminine Heart:

When we laugh and cry together
The salt and the sweet blend together
creating a special elixir
that we share with one another.
Sisters in this life,
We have come to share
our love and beauty.
We acknowledge that beauty
by holding up mirrors
for one another.
Your Spirit is so beautiful,
I tell a friend without words.
She smiles and radiates
love and light.
My heartfelt gratitude to Goddess
for the loving gift of girlfriends.

Nothing heals a broken heart like time and girlfriends.
— GWYNETH PALTROW —

ONE OF THE MOST COMMON COMPLAINTS I hear from women is that they don't have enough time to relax and enjoy their girlfriends.

Many women feel they don't have enough time to play with their kids, enough intimate time with their partners, or enough time to be alone. Often our friendships with our girlfriends suffer because of it. We suffer as well because one of the most healing things we can do for ourselves is to spend time with other women with whom we can laugh or cry.

Participating in women-only events has a special energy that is different from the energy at functions attended by both men and women. Whether the event is an all-woman sleepover or a gathering of women celebrating the birth of a child, the sharing between women is a special form of sisterhood.

The intention of these gatherings and celebrations is not about, "What can we do that won't involve the men?" Rather, it is about, "What can we do that will fill our hearts with love and joy, then let us share that joy with others?" Ever notice how much more appreciation you and your partner have for the wonderful woman that you are after you spend some quality time sharing deeply with the girls?

We need the comfort and support of our female friends to help kindle the spirit we share within. The love and nurturing that the daughters of light share with one another is of a very high frequency. We get activated on all levels when we allow our full feminine expression with others of the same intention. We grow in the presence of love. The reflections we offer in our radiance further ignite the light in others.

The love and nurturing that the daughters of light share with one another is of a very high frequency.

Being with other women in celebration can be a transformational experience, if you attend with an open heart. Heaven knows that a heart-sharing session with the girls can change lives. It is cheap therapy, too! Honestly sharing yourself helps you verbalize those crazy feelings and emotions whirling around in your mind, so that you can begin to make sense of them. If you feel love from your friends, listen to their advice.

One of the best medicines for the Feminine Heart is to be in a warm, nurturing environment with your girlfriends. This can heal a host of ills, from re-connecting with your deep feminine essence to warming your heart and bringing back that radiant smile and light into your eyes. A girls' night out laughing, talking, eating delectable delights, dancing, singing and sharing trials and tribulations can be terrific medicine, especially when you've been singing the blues.

When we are lighthearted with our girlfriends, we talk more. Laughing becomes easier. As we relax into our feelings, we become more physically animated. Too much of a good thing, however, does not serve. If your only encounters with girlfriends involve partying and having a good time, you are missing the point.

Going to a nightclub and yelling above the music while sucking in cigarette fumes and waiting for some undeserving half-drunk man to ask you to dance is not what I had in mind. Although it may be a reminder of your hormonal drives of yesterday, it will not do much to soften you into your Feminine Heart, or to feed your Spirit. It is like eating junk food — you put food into your body, but the experience isn't satisfying or healthy.

One of the 10 Commandments is to love your neighbor as you love yourself. We are on this planet for such a brief time. Many people come through our lives, and we are given opportunities to interact with many different souls. The enlightened woman discriminates. You would be wise to choose your friends from those with the highest thoughts, so that their light is reflected back at you.

It takes time to attract new friends. Give yourself this time. Friendships are the sweet nectar of life. Sip slowly … Enjoy them. We attract our mirrors. Kind hearts attract other kind hearts. If you live as the divine feminine, you will attract other divine friends. Choose wisely. Most important, find friends whose values reflect yours. When you lower your ideals, you create an anxiousness that can deplete your energy. At the same time, do not exclude anyone from your love.

Be a friend to all, but remember that not everyone may be ready for your friendship. You must build a solid foundation, so that your friendships can flourish on a base built on the *Friendships are the sweet nectar of life. Sip slowly … Enjoy them.* trust of unconditional love. Most people are looking to gain something from others. Never give up your freedoms, ideals or wisdom for self-gain, but rather hold tight to your principles as an enlightened woman.

Having some one-on-one time with a special girlfriend is also good medicine. One of the best forms of therapy is a heartfelt conversation with a good friend. A girlfriend who knows and trusts you can often be there for you when you need to talk over important issues in your life. Unlike our intimate partners, girlfriends do not create the same reactions and hurts, or hit our weak spots, quite like our men.

We are in each other's lives to heal. Giving and receiving friendship is indeed a gift of the Feminine Heart. People enter and exit our lives all the time. Whether friends are there for a reason, a season or a lifetime, it is the loving and the learning that happens while we are together that is important.

Letting go of friendships is often painful. We realize that we have outgrown someone, or perhaps the quality of our exchanges no longer serves our Higher Selves. When a friendship no longer supports us in keeping our hearts open to loving experiences, we may have to re-evaluate our motivation for spending time with the other person.

That is where girlfriends come in. Nothing will get you back into your feminine side more quickly and deeply than spending some good, quality time having fun with your female friends. Dance and sing until your hearts explode with love and laughter.

Musings & Blessings

WHEN WAS THE LAST TIME YOU CRIED TEARS OF JOY from a shared sense of spontaneous delight? Do you have a healthy balance between being with people out of obligation, duty or responsibility, and sharing time with your girlfriends just for the sheer joy of it?

Femininity begets femininity.

Celebrate and enjoy. Dance around a fire, or dance in your living room. Just dance. Dance with each other in celebration of the love that you are. Sharing the love and beauty of your femininity with other women is a gift that gives back. Femininity begets femininity. Sharing your Feminine Heart with other like-hearted women is good medicine. Laugh, cry, breathe, sing and dance.

My friends are my estate.
— EMILY DICKINSON —

The Gift of Healing

My Darling Feminine Heart:

I feel the pain and suffering
in and around me.
I have so much to share
that can heal the ills of the earth.
Take my hands and with my heart
put them to good use.
May all my thoughts and actions
be used for good and healing.
With humble thanks to Spirit
the Goddess doctor behind all healing.

The influence of each human being on others in this life is a kind of immortality.
— JOHN QUINCY ADAMS —

WOMEN ARE NATURAL HEALERS. We have the ability to heal with our love whenever we choose. We can open our hearts to varying degrees, depending on our level of understanding and our ability to surrender. Both require learning and practice.

The resurgence of women entering the fields of alternative medicine and the ancient healing arts shows our natural inclination to serve others. Many women have had their own health issues, and this has given them an appreciation for good health. Or they have watched people they love suffer when their lives were compromised due to health issues. We have a natural desire to help others with our knowledgeable and compassionate hearts.

To truly heal another, we must first heal ourselves. Any thoughts and actions that don't contribute to our well-being, or that of others, is energy wasted. Our first responsibility is to heal ourselves. Only then can we offer the best of who we are to others.

Every time we board an airplane, we are reminded to put on our oxygen masks first and then take care of those around us. When we breathe in the life force that gives us our healing and vitality, we have so much more to offer our loved ones.

AS A YOUNG WOMAN I began to see the correlation between my health challenges and my thoughts and emotions. When I became stressed out during final exams, or emotionally deranged during a breakup with a boyfriend, I inevitably came down with a cold or the flu. Was it a coincidence? I began to question the power of my thoughts as they related to my well-being, and I studied the health of those people around me.

I saw my maternal grandmother, Annie, succumb to cancer of the tongue and neck, leading into her shoulder. One thing I found frustrating was that she never spoke up for herself, even if my grandfather spoke rudely to her. A hardworking Ukrainian woman, she would never talk against my grandfather, no matter what he said or did. The surgeons continued to cut away the diseased areas, but she had a strong mind and a will to live. After half her tongue had been cut out and the cancer had spread down her neck and into her shoulder, I had to say something.

"Please say something to him when he gets like that, Grandma. You're killing yourself!"

I told her this on different occasions, in different ways. She would look at me with sad eyes, but she always did what she thought best. This wonderful woman taught me many things about health, about love and about life. Watching her fall prey to the insidious disease of cancer confirmed so much about the power of our thoughts and emotions to heal or harm our physical bodies.

The next condition she developed was a benign tremor. During the latter stages she could not feed herself, as her shaking hands would throw the food all over the place before it ever got to her mouth. I felt that her body was shaking from holding on to so much that she was unwilling to express, that it was literally trying to come out even as she held on tightly, trying to keep everything bottled up inside. It broke my heart. She would never understand, even if I tried to explain my observations and understanding.

After watching my grandmother suffer, much to the dismay of a few men I decided that I would not remain unexpressed when it came to matters of the heart. My health was too important.

When your Feminine Heart does not honor herself, there is an inner suffering. Most women are highly intuitive, especially about their own feelings. Sometimes heaviness creeps in and around our hearts, much like a cloud slowly blocking the light of the sun. Like the tides that change with the phases of the moon, the tides of our feminine emotions are affected by the extent of the love and light that we give and receive.

Anyone who has feared for his or her life *without health we have nothing.* because of health issues knows that without health we have nothing. Neither love nor money can make up for losing one's health for most people. Life pales when we lose our health or vitality. Soon we filter all our thoughts through the reality called "I'm sick." Reversing the progression takes effort. Often it requires a change of thought and action.

If it is part of our destiny, we will be given opportunities to challenge our beliefs about sickness, health and healing through our life experiences.

The following story illustrates the journey that I had to take to realize that Spirit will never let us down when we are willing to allow its presence in our life.

W HEN I WAS 21, traveling in Mexico en route to Guatemala to study Spanish, I met a couple of young men doing an expedition into the heart of the Mexican jungle. They invited me to join them. I had been traveling alone, and was happy to have the company of a couple of interesting and accomplished young men.

One night while we were sleeping in our hammocks hanging from the trees deep alongside the waterfalls at Aqua Azul, a torrential storm blew in. It was the middle of the night, and we got soaked. Tired and cold, we needed to find shelter. Ahead in the distance we could see a fire burning. Trudging through the jungle with our sopping wet gear in hand, we forged our way to a fire warming a Mexican campesino family.

The man of the family walked towards us as we came near their humble jungle home. In broken Spanish we explained our situation, and he invited us to join his family sleeping on the ground around the fire. Chickens walked around while the fire beckoned. We were grateful to have a warm spot to lay our heads until dawn. After a couple of hours of fitful sleep we awoke with the sun, thanked our gracious host, and went back to our camping spot to collect the rest of our belongings.

Weeks passed. A big pimple appeared on my left cheek. While going through puberty I had had the usual pimple breakouts before my periods, but I never had a pimple like this one. As the days passed and it didn't go away, but continued to grow into a big bump on my face, I became scared. Intuitively, I knew that something was amiss. I began the long process of finding a medical person who knew what was growing on my face.

I heard it all. Every medical place that I visited had a different diagnosis — acne, a blocked sebaceous gland. Everyone was an expert. I was prescribed everything from antibiotics to sap from a certain tree that the local people used for healing skin problems. Still I felt lousy. Emotionally, I was scared. The bump on my cheek caved in, leaving a big wet lesion the size of a 50-cent piece in the middle of my cheek. Some nights I would wake up screaming, seeing my body riddled with holes. I knew that something was eating at my skin and flesh. I could feel it.

Finally, I met a doctor who seemed to know what he was looking at. "I can't help you," he said sternly, "But my son can. He is a specialist in tropical diseases and he will know what disease you have." I was grateful. Finally I had hope and confidence that I had found help.

Dr. Renato Soto Pacheco was a handsome young doctor. He took one look at my face and knew exactly what was going on. "You have parasites living in your face that are eating the flesh," he said. "Leishmaniasis is fairly uncommon these days. It is a parasite transmitted by small sand flies that live on birds and animals in the jungle." My heart fell. It was those damned chickens. That fateful night around the fire. It all came back to me.

"There is a medicine manufactured in France that can help with this disease," he said. "It requires you to have a shot of medicine in your hip every 12 hours for 12 days. This will kill the parasite."

I nodded. What choice did I have? He told me that if the parasite spread from my cheek into my nose, eyes or ears it could enter my whole body, and that it could be fatal.

"When can we start the procedure?" I asked.

"Now," he replied.

For the next twelve days we met twice a day. I bared my hip and he shoved in a big needle filled with some kind of solution that poisoned the parasites living in my face. Unfortunately, it killed a lot more than just the parasites. In my bloodstream, the toxic substance killed other things along the way. I got very sick. My hair started falling out in clumps. I had terrible stomach pains. My ovaries and kidneys became infected. In short, I was a mess. But slowly, slowly, the dripping wetness in the hole in my face started drying up.

Throughout this process I started to pray fervently. If there was a God, surely he would hear my prayers and heal me of this disfiguring disease before it got the best of me. After I started to regain my strength, I headed back to Canada. Weak and tired, I was in no shape to continue traveling. I had been away from my family and friends for almost a year and I longed for the comforts of home.

When I arrived on my family's doorstep, everyone was in shock. They tried to hide their horror at seeing my face, but I could read their eyes. Nevertheless, they were happy that I was home. Within a short time of arriving back in Canada, I noticed a wet liquid seeping out of the wound that hadn't totally healed. I was devastated. I still had those damn parasites.

I went to my family physician, who wanted to give me chemotherapy. "Forget it!" I said. My mother contacted the Centre for Travel and Tropical Medicine in Toronto. At that time, the Centre wasn't familiar with treating this disease. Once again, I called my doctor by phone, and told him of my plight.

"Unfortunately, the drug manufacturer has stopped producing the serum you need," he informed me quietly, in a strong Spanish accent. There was a stunned silence. "I do have a partial box of vials. A couple of them have broken, but I am happy to send them if you are willing to give them a try."

It was a mixed blessing. The effects of the last treatment were worse than the actual disease.

"Send them up," I said, determined to conquer those little carnivores.

Within two weeks the package arrived. My sister, a nurse, administered the shots. This time, however, I was determined not to let the drug affect the rest of my body. I decided to go on a juice fast using fresh vegetables that helped support the liver in detoxifying the body. Cabbage, broccoli, alfalfa sprouts and myriad other foul-tasting veggie juices became my sustenance while going through the course of treatment.

I shut myself off from friends and family, and focused on healing. I started to pray — a lot. One day, something compelled me to get out of hiding and to go to the local library. I walked over to the religion section and pulled down a book that seemed to jump off the shelf at me. It was a book on Sanskrit prayers. Opening the book, my eyes rested on a passage about how we can heal ourselves when we keep our thoughts on God.

Healing was something I desperately wanted. I borrowed the book and read it as soon as I got home. The essence of its message was that when we keep our hearts connected to God through prayer, healing takes place. I chose a short Sanskrit prayer that translated into English as, "I am one with God."

I told my family not to disturb me and went into hibernation. Like a monk hidden away in a dark cave, I prayed and meditated on those words. When other thoughts streamed in I would automatically replace them with my little prayer. All my waking hours I repeated this prayer in my mind's eye. It became so ingrained in me that even when I woke up in the middle of the night my mind was reciting the prayer that occupied all my thoughts during the day.

I began to feel a sense of peace and clarity. My fear dissipated. I was alone, yet I felt so connected to my Creator. Without the distractions of the everyday world, my mind became free. I knew that I had the power to heal myself using God's presence in my life.

Allowing Spirit's healing love into my life deeply changed how I saw the world. One cold January day I decided to go out for a walk. Above the crunching of the hard snow, I heard a small sparrow calling out to me in song. I looked up at that tiny bird, and he spoke to me. My mind was so clear that I could hear his message. "You and I are one," it sang. My heart was filled with joy. So few words had passed between me and other living creatures in the previous few weeks. This was the sweetest message I could have heard.

At that moment, I got it. I realized that when we go deep inside ourselves the Spirit residing within is the same Spirit residing in all living creatures. I was in awe of that little bird, that messenger of the truth. "Thank you," was all I said. My life had been forever changed. I now knew that the only separation between me and all of life was the imposition of mind. That little bird shared with me a lesson that has served me to this day.

MANY PEOPLE MUST FACE A HEALING CRISIS AT SOME POINT. Rather than focus on the disease, shift your attention to the gift being offered to you. Disease demands immediate attention. If you accept your condition as an opportunity to learn where you need to make some changes, it may be the best thing that has ever happened. Healing can occur on many levels — spiritual, emotional and physical. When we become disconnected to Spirit, our emotions suffer and ultimately our pain and suffering manifests as dis-ease in our physical bodies.

All healing begins with Spirit. When we open our Feminine Hearts to love, we can begin to heal ourselves of many of our physical ailments.

Musings & Blessings

HOW CAN YOU HEAL YOURSELF AND OTHERS in little ways, every day? Let your heart be light. What fills your radiant heart to the brim? Spend more time doing those things instead of vacuuming or doing the laundry — unless of course, that is your deepest gift. You are the embodiment of our Creator's divine expression. You can heal others — and yourself — with the gift of love.

When an illness is a part of your spiritual journey, no medical intervention can heal you until your spirit has begun to make the changes that the illness was designed to inspire.
— CAROLINE MYSS, PhD —

The Gift of Heritage

My Darling Feminine Heart:

I don't have to travel far
to see my grandmother's peasant hands
or my mother's thick, healthy hair.
I look in the mirror and see
many of my people
who walked before me.
I don't remember them except
for their stories
and the odd photograph.
Who was that young
man who fell in love
with my mother?
They have left their legacies
in their stories, their quilts,
their values, and their children.
They left behind meaning
that helps to make sense
of my life.
Thank you, Goddess, for reminding me
where I came from.

Good parents give their children roots and wings.
Roots to know where home is,
wings to fly away and exercise what's been taught them.
— Jonas Salk —

IN THIS TIME OF MOBILITY AND THE DISSOLUTION OF THE FAMILY STRUCTURE, our heritage is becoming more difficult to preserve. Yet more than ever our future generations need to know that they have roots from which they can blossom.

If we are to build a solid life, a strong foundation is essential. We can choose to change our circumstances throughout life, but having an awareness of our heritage gives us strength to draw on. When we have knowledge of our heritage we feel connected to the larger part of life.

Our Feminine Heart is the gatekeeper of heritage. The stories we tell, the traditions we practice, and the food we serve all reflect the heritage we were given. The kinds of foods you serve to your family, and your method of preparation, is often learned from your mother or grandmother. Your values, your way of responding to things in life, have been passed on by those who came before you.

My grandmother showed her love by making sure there were large amounts of well-prepared and tasty meals served regularly.

"Eat, eat!" she would command.

"But Grandma, I'm not hungry!" I would protest, much to her dismay.

"But you gonna be hungry!" she would say adamantly.

My mother continued this tradition with me, and now I find that I have passed it on to my son.

My grandmother's parents came from Eastern Europe in the early 1890s to break and settle the free land that the Canadian government was offering to immigrants. She knew what hungry meant.

Grandma grew big, fat, juicy strawberries that she served with fresh cream from a cow she had milked, cream so thick a spoon would stand up in it. Several varieties of fresh tomatoes sliced thinly and served with sweet, crisp cucumbers were a daily offering on her summer table. Her creamy coconut pie with a flaky crust that came out of her wood-fired oven was to die for! This was a woman who lived to nurture her family with food from the earth. The love that she put into her food sustained our family in so many ways.

She grew almost all her own food. She planted with her heart and the promise that at the end of the growing season her family would be rewarded with fresh, wholesome food. There was always more than enough. Sacks of potatoes and other vegetables were given to other families and to the church in abundance.

As a culture, we have distanced ourselves from the agrarian way of life only to find that we have distanced ourselves from ourselves.

Respect for Mother Earth is part of the heritage we must pass on to our children if they are to respect her bounties and look after her best interests. Not every woman needs to have her own garden plot to connect with the miracles that the earth provides us. But as enlightened women, we must learn to respect and appreciate Mother Earth to fully honor and respect ourselves.

Some of the things you can implement as part of your daily life to reduce the stress on Mother Earth include the following:

- Recycle paper, glass and other items.
- Nurture real plants in your home, to remind you of the wonder and beauty of nature.
- If you have access to even a small piece of turf, throw in a few lettuce, spinach, Swiss chard and radish seeds, just to experience the bounty of the earth. If you are an apartment dweller, you can do this on your balcony,
- If you have children, start an avocado tree from the pit of an avocado or start any other fast-growing plant. This will help children understand how things grow.
- When possible, shop at local farmers' markets and fresh food stands to treat your taste buds to locally grown food. The difference in the quality of food that hasn't been transported for days or weeks from another part of the planet is remarkable.

TRADITIONS ARE ANOTHER PART OF OUR HERITAGE that would rarely happen in the home without feminine energy. The way we celebrate the special passages of life: birth, birthdays, anniversaries and religious and cultural holidays, all hold special significance. These occasions can influence family members for generations, depending on how they are celebrated in the home.

My mother always celebrated our birthdays with a special cake she had made. Christmas was a time of tremendous celebration, with specially prepared food and goodies that magically appeared only at this special time of year. She transformed our home into a sparkling wonderland, even when she had very few resources at hand.

The memories we make are what our loved ones take into the future. If you don't already do so, start with small celebrations or traditions that are meaningful to you and your family. Include input from your family members — what activities do they enjoy that could become part of your own family traditions. These same traditions may eventually be shared by the families of your children's children.

Along with traditions, our heritage is shared most memorably in the stories of our past, and the histories of family members who have come before us. Many of our ancestors did not record their life experiences, and it is only through their oral stories that we have threads from the past to connect the fabric of our lives.

Years ago, before my grandfather passed away, I recorded many stories of his life that nobody had ever heard. I remember asking him why he chose to marry my grandmother, instead of all the other women he knew. I had visions of him watching her across a meadow filled with beautiful wildflowers, and falling in love with her feminine beauty.

"She was the hardest worker I knew," he told me matter-of-factly. This was a big part of my heritage, yet I would never have known it without taking the time to ask and to listen. It has given me insights into who I am today. Knowing and sharing our heritage is an important piece of the puzzle — it helps us to understand, accept and love who we are and where we came from.

Take the time to talk to your elders and family members. They hold secrets from the past that may help you unlock some of the mysteries of the present. Ask them questions about their lives and their loves, then share your new-found knowledge with your family. Heritage is a bond that helps keep family together. Without this knowledge, pieces of our lives are lost forever.

Collect things from the past that have meaning to your cultural heritage, and talk about them with your family. Where did they come from? How did you end up owning them? Display those beautifully painted Ukrainian Easter eggs, your collection of African masks, or your grandmother's antique Chinese tea set.

When your Feminine Heart acknowledges the people, places and things from her past, she is calling in the love and nurturing of her ancestors and their heritage. They grow with us and through us.

Musings & Blessings

WHEN WAS THE LAST TIME YOU CELEBRATED A SPECIAL OCCASION? Did you include elements that can become a tradition in your home with your family and friends? What is the heritage you wish to leave behind, knowing that it may be cherished for years to come?

Include your family members in making new traditions. What will they remember long after you are gone? Will your Royal Doulton china be remembered as something that sat in a china cabinet because it was too good to be used often? Or will your family remember the chips on the teacups as part of the celebrations of good food shared in merriment?

Breathe in all that you know is good and loving about your heritage. Exhale the betrayal, sadness and dysfunction of the past. Breathe in love … just breathe.

To be ignorant of what occurred before you were born is to remain always a child.
For what is the worth of human life, unless it is woven into the life
of our ancestors by the records of history?
— CICERO —

The Gift of Intimacy

My Darling Feminine Heart:

As I wrap my heart's tendrils
around your delicate Spirit
I sniff the sweet scent
of love as it passes
through my heart's open door.
Your heart is softened
when it touches mine.
Together we massage
each other's Spirits,
with love and trust.
Thank you Goddess,
for the delicious gift
of intimacy.

To love is first of all to accept yourself as you actually are.
– Thich Nhat Hanh –

I COULD READ THEIR THOUGHTS. The furtive glances. The body language clearly signaling judgments people were making about each other.

"This guy is too short. That woman is too fat. This person isn't dressed how I like my men to dress. No one in this room is worth getting to know." People would check each other out and, after forming an opinion based on a snap judgment, distance themselves. They wouldn't even bother coming up to introduce themselves.

My challenge was to get the participants to connect with the others in the room, to move beyond superficial judgments. The exercise I came up with was designed to get everyone looking more deeply into each other. This involved forming two circles, women on the inside and men on the outside. I asked the men to stand firmly, with their feet planted securely on the floor. With their feet grounded, they opened up their chests by breathing slowly and purposefully. This helped connect them to the earth.

The women were also encouraged to breathe. I wanted them to relax the tight muscles and pinched faces, and to open up to love. When you take a few deep breaths, you can feel the tension leave your body, preparing your heart for love. It is difficult to feel uptight and to have an open heart at the same time.

Here was the challenge I gave the women: surrender your heart to the masculine stranger standing in front of you. Breathe deeply, and let your body go soft. Release any tension you feel. Breathe in love, letting go of anything that doesn't look or feel like love.

With hesitancy and some resistance, men facing inward and women looking outward, the participants went deeper and deeper into themselves. The intent was to get the men and women to experience sexual essence — their own, and that of the opposite sex — as well as to experience their own sexual power. A number of the exercises helped the men feel strong and masculine, while other exercises helped the women become radiant beings who gave and received love. Masculine and feminine sexual essence is available for everyone to experience.

Looking deeply into the eyes of the person opposite them, just breathing, without expectations and without judgment, the participants let themselves into each other's hearts. Standing in front of a woman, each man was asked to say, "The beauty I see in you is…" He would state something he saw in the deep pools of her eyes. Diving into the moist abyss of her eyes with all his masculine presence, the man shared his steadfast gaze, gently inviting the woman to trust him and to let him into her heart. In turn, the woman breathed deeply, silently taking in the man's undivided attention.

Again he said, "The beauty I see in you is …" and again the receptive woman took in his caring observation and let another wave of delight wash over her.

Next, looking across at the man in front of her, each woman in her deep radiance said, "I know I can trust you because…" She would finish this statement with something she felt to be true about the man. Breathing him deeply into her heart and softening her body, relaxing and allowing her heart to open up, she repeated the statement, again finishing it with something she felt to be true.

After several minutes of opening up in this way, the men and women rated their partners on how radiant or trustworthy they felt them to be. After receiving the rating, the partners thanked each other and the outer circle of men took a step to the right until each stood in front of the next woman. And so it went, until the circle was completed.

Sharing the beauty each man saw in the wonderful feminine creature standing before him was a gift to the receiving woman. As the women took in words they knew to be true about themselves, I could see them softening.

The power of this exercise was extraordinary! The men relished the opportunity to feel filled by the love that was there for them. The women, on the other hand, were charged up by staring into the eyes of a man who they knew they could trust, whose presence was like a solid rock. They felt free to express themselves, and to let go of any place in their body that they were clenching closed. They could do this because in front of them was a solid man whose direction was clear, whose vision was honorable, and whose presence was unflinching.

This is a gift to the Feminine Heart. Being in the presence of a man whose thoughts, actions and vision are unwavering is a delight to the feminine. It is a complete turn-on for women, as it is an experience of freedom. She can trust her man to stay on course with his purpose, which allows her the freedom to fully express her ever-changing and flowing emotional range, without guilt.

The amount of love generated in that room was indescribable. This group of seemingly unconnected men and women created a space of honor, respect and pure love for the other sex. Some people melted and fell in love with each other. For the first time, many participants experienced a pure kind of love for everyone they met. In fact, several women told me afterward that the love they felt was enough to convince them to marry many of the men in that room. Quite a shift from the beginning of the weekend.

What took place was not sexual attraction — not superficial attraction or attraction based only on the outer physical aspects. By going deeper and sensing who their partner was at his or her core, the participants saw the truth of each other's being, and an incredible intimacy was shared.

WHEN WE ACKNOWLEDGE THE GIFT OF INTIMACY WITH PURE INTENTION, the Feminine Heart responds and intuitively sees who the other person is, without having prior knowledge about the person. One of the greatest gifts you can give another person is to be a mirror, where the other person sees his or her own divinity in you. We know that this person is a child of God, too. We are the same. We are one. This is the basis of real intimacy.

When two people share themselves authentically, they create a space where true intimacy can take place. Once we've had the real thing, there is little satisfaction in relationships where only the outer shell of the person is experienced. Without feeling the heart and sensing the soul of our partners, we can only partake of the most superficial aspects of intimacy.

Becoming vulnerable and letting another person see us for who we are requires us to dispose of facades and affectations. The reward for dropping our props and jettisoning the stories we tell others, however, far outweighs the empty results of keeping up false appearances. There is no intimacy like that of witnessing the pure Spirit of love in another.

Share the truth of who you are. Share your Spirit as well as your body. Allow yourself to expand into the space of all life. Allow yourself just to *be*. This will allow the other person to feel safe in your presence. When your partner knows that you are non-judgmental, you give that person the freedom to *be* as well. You honor that deep place where you are one with the Spirit of life. Do not destroy that opportunity. Do not ignore the face of love.

It's all about surrendering that big, beautiful heart of yours to the people who pass by. Do not fight, resist or reject their love — if it's pure and of good intention, embrace it and give back.

This book has grown out of our deep need for intimacy. For us to access intimacy with others, we must first have an intimate relationship with ourselves. To experience a deep relationship with ourselves, we must have an intimate connection to our Source, the connection of love with the oneness of life.

WHEN YOU ARE CONNECTED TO YOUR HIGHER SELF, you will connect deeply with others. This is the human experience. The quality of this experience will determine your experiences in life, personally and professionally.

Working with both men and women, the masculine and the feminine, I found that there are differences in how we experience others and ourselves. From a biological and emotional point of view, men and women are very different. Psychological research has shown for years that human beings have both masculine and feminine aspects. What the research shows is that approximately 80 per cent of women have a predominantly feminine sexual identity, and approximately 80 per cent of men have a predominantly masculine sexual nature.

Energy in relationships is always balanced. As a woman, if you spend most of your time focused on attaining goals and meeting deadlines, you will most likely attract a more feminine male partner, a partner who is more concerned with depth of feelings, with the state of the relationship, and with bringing beauty and grace into your surroundings. If you want to attract a more masculine partner in your life, you must embrace more of your own feminine qualities.

Nothing soothes the rough edges around our hearts more quickly than an intimate connection with another human being. Whether the connection is made through an intimate gaze or a gentle touch, deep connection with others gives one a profound sense of self. The effect is of being part of the whole of humanity.

THE RAPID PACE AT WHICH MANY PEOPLE RUN THEIR LIVES leaves little time for intimate connections. The Feminine Heart must take the time to experience intimacy for her greatest desire to be realized — to give and receive love. Do not overlook the opportunities where you can make an intimate contribution to others — in the process fulfilling your desires and serving your creator.

In this high-tech world we are surrounded by people in crowded cities, but there is more loneliness and alienation than ever. We don't have to go far to see the need for intimate connection etched upon the faces of people as they pass by on the streets. We can see the pain of people who crave the experience of being connected to others at a deep level. The Feminine Heart is sensitive to the pain of strangers who she has never met. The pain on people's faces, and the sadness emanating from their hearts, fills her with heaviness.

When you are born, you are complete in your openness to life and to love. You know only love, and you are free in your expression of love, pleasure and displeasure. It doesn't take long before you are told that you are not a "good" girl if you behave in a certain manner. You start to separate yourself from your birthright as a child of God.

When life provides you with experience after experience, when you come to believe that you are not perfect in your entirety, you begin to protect your loving Feminine Heart. You start to protect yourself from others so that they cannot hurt you, so that they cannot see your imperfections. As children, you tell lies so that others will not think you are bad. As adults, you continue to tell lies — to yourself and to others — about your imperfections. Any message that you communicate to others, or to yourself, that says, "I am not perfect in my expression as a daughter of our creator," is a lie.

You are perfect. But what you choose to express is sometimes less than Goddess-like. When you buy into your own stories about your imperfection, they cost you dearly. They cost you your health, your happiness, and your feminine radiance.

Sarah Ban Breathnach, in her book *Something More*, describes the feeling of sadness and pain we experience in daily life as "divine discontent." You know when there is major dissatisfaction in your life. Something is working under the surface, showing that you are not living up to your highest expression of truth.

At some point everyone is a stranger to everyone else, but in reality we are all One. When you have direct experience of your own divinity you can see the divinity in others and, in turn, their divinity becomes apparent to them. You are mirrors for each other's Spirit. This is the gift of intimacy that you offer to each other. Your challenge is to bring this gift into all aspects of your life — to not only fulfill your desires, but to serve others in the best way you can.

Author Marianne Williamson expressed it this way in her book, *Enchanted Love*: "Enchanted intimacy bestows a shared ministry, a common mission of two souls in service to a force that is bigger than either one. We are separate and we are one as well — indeed, as is all humanity. It is time to live as if our oneness mattered."

Many women anesthetize themselves so that they don't fully feel the need to connect deeply with other human beings. To erase the deep ache of loneliness, they fill themselves up with food, with alcohol, with shopping, or with any number of other distractions. In our fast-paced world, there are many opportunities to connect with others, but in our crowded cities the eyes of the strangers who pass by are averted, for fear that they may harm us if we let them get too close. We want and need closeness and intimate connection with others, yet we put up barriers against easily experiencing intimacy.

In your daily life you may be surrounded by hundreds of people yet feel alone, craving the closeness and intimacy of contact from people with whom you feel safe. This is such a deep and profound need that studies have shown that babies left alone without touch or human connection will not develop normally, and may even have severe developmental disabilities.

You may remember a time when you agreed to a sexual encounter beyond what your heart told you was appropriate because you so yearned for intimacy and connection with another human being. You are not alone. Being touched is a huge need in our high-tech world. Your kids need to be touched to develop properly. The Feminine Heart aches to feel herself connected to others — physically, emotionally and Spiritually. Even animals crave contact with other living creatures.

If your intention is one of kindness and healing, your act of intimacy toward someone will be received in good faith. What is your intention in giving the gift of intimacy? This will determine the manner in which it is received.

Many a woman has become dispirited when she realizes that her man can't, or won't, open up his heart. Many, many divorces and broken relationships are a result of this lack of heart-centered connection. When the feminine essence starts shutting her heart down, everything else follows. Her loving becomes shallow and edgy. Sexual energy may become darker, or more manipulative. The once-delicious caresses and kisses become less juicy and healing for everyone involved.

The feminine tendency to express feelings is natural. The masculine often interprets this as "complaining." It depends upon your attitude, perspective and intention.

"He isn't a good communicator," or "He only talks about himself and never asks me about me," or "He doesn't like to dance," or "He is too controlling," or "He isn't there for me," or "He spends too much money." These are just some of the more common complaints I've heard while discussing the reason for the breakup of my client's last marriage or serious relationship.

Working with women, I intuitively know that the reasons they give are almost always symptoms of that lack of a deep heart connection. They are not feeling connected with their Higher Selves, so they blame it on their man (or on anything else in the vicinity).

Musings & Blessings

WHAT'S AN ENLIGHTENED WOMAN TO DO to deeply melt into love's bliss? You have choices. You can open yourself up further to support your partner opening his heart, you can spend some quality time by yourself in meditation or in nature, or you can go dancing with your girlfriends. You have many choices. Do the things that allow you to feel most intimately connected to yourself first, and then intimacy with others will flow easily.

Breathe in your intimate connection with "The Divine Mother" herself. Let go … exhale anything that doesn't look or feel like love. Breathe in love.

Whatever you do, if you do it sincerely,
will eventually become a bridge to your wholeness,
a good ship that carries you through the darkness.
– CARL JUNG –

The Gift of Intuition

My Darling Feminine Heart:

I knew when you tugged
on my heartstrings,
then kicked me in the stomach,
that you were trying to get my attention.
I heard you,
but I didn't listen.
I'm a slow learner sometimes.
Have patience
I'm working at trusting
myself.
Thank you, Goddess, for revealing my Higher Self
knowing that I can believe in it.

In the heart of every human being lies hid the flower of the intuition.
— ALICE BAILEY —

ENLIGHTENED WOMEN THROUGHOUT THE AGES trusted their intuition as a matter of survival. They knew when to leave a place, where to find food, and who to trust with critical skills. There were no telephones or emails providing continuous communication about the state of a war in a neighboring village, or about the feeling in a lover's heart.

In today's scientific, rational and analytical world, however, we have come to discredit information that seems to come out of nowhere. "We want the facts, not a lot of hogwash about feelings," is a common line, as though our feelings don't have any credibility. As a result, we push them down, down, down until we don't feel anything anymore.

Working with women over the years, this is the one area I see squelched out of them. The more successful a woman is in the business world, the more I hear, "I just don't know what I feel any more."

The definition of intuition, according to Webster's dictionary, is: "Immediate apprehension or cognition, the power or faculty of attaining to direct knowledge without rational inference." Another more metaphysical definition, according to author Alice Bailey, is "apprehension of reality exactly as it is."

No matter how you define it, most people just say, "I don't know how I know, I just know" or "I feel something in my gut." It's good that we are aware of what's going on in our bodies. As women, we must be empowered to re-embrace our innate capacities, to become more of who we really are. As we move into a new world order we can see the limitations of logic, rationality and our current left-brain, rational way of thinking. The results are obvious. When we look around at the state of the planet, we can easily see how the more masculine-linear way of thinking affects how we live.

In her book *Practical Intuition*, author Laura Day describes how the over-reliance on linear thought is a relatively recent phenomenon whose greatest proponent was the French philosopher René Descartes. Descartes carried on an intellectual tradition that had roots in ancient Greece — the birthplace of logic and the rudiments of the scientific method. It was also the land of the Delphic Oracle, Day concludes, where rational thought was recognized as incomplete without the support of intuition.

My intention here is not to weigh you down in philosophical history, but to speak to you as an enlightened woman about something you already know but perhaps have forgotten — your intuition is a tool that serves you when you use it consciously. Most of us already use it unconsciously, so this is an opportunity to see how we can turn up the volume. Intuition is something that we are already getting results from — and we can get even greater results.

Our intuition taps into the source of wisdom, knowledge and information that lies just below the surface of conscious awareness. Carl Jung, a noted psychoanalyst, called this level of mind the "collective unconscious" although it has since been given various other names. The information and wisdom collected since the dawn of woman's emergence on the planet is held in this place. You have access to that cumulative wisdom when you so desire.

Although intuition may manifest itself in feelings and sensations, it doesn't just come out of nowhere. Science has shown that we have information stored in our bodies at a cellular level that contains memory from our ancestors. Since birth, our bodies and brains have stored information in much the same way that a computer stores data.

Intuition however, separates human thinking from computer-like reasoning. Although it is based on information stored in our minds, intuition skips the conscious steps. It appears suddenly as a gut feeling. Because it is based on facts, it is often not wrong. But if we doubt our feelings, we cannot access the innate gift that is there for us to use.

Sometimes the decision may seem inconsequential. "Should I buy the little red dress with the interesting neckline, or the exquisite backless black dress with sequins." Other decisions have more serious, life-long consequences. "Should I accept this man's marriage proposal after knowing him only two months — even though I've never felt so sure about anything in my life?"

In either case we go inside, looking for the right answer, trusting our Higher Selves to make a sound decision. I know that to skeptics this sounds too simple to be workable, but to the enlightened woman who has experience with intuition, it is very feasible.

Here is one way of doing it. Whenever you have a puzzling situation that needs an immediate solution, stop what you are doing and for a moment go into a "mindless" state. Be aware of your thoughts in this moment. Still your mind. Breathe the life force deeply into your being. Exhale. Feel that space between breaths. Live in that calm, quiet space, and just *be*.

Continue until you feel loved, nurtured, centered and calm. Take that feeling with you as you inhale your next breath. Exhale. The breath of life is what sustains. Breathe intentionally, letting go of any constrictions.

This "non-thinking" state can last for as long as you feel comfortable, which for most people is up to one minute. It may help to focus your attention if you look out the window at the limitless sky, or if you set your eyes on a white wall, or on a flickering candle. Anything neutral that suspends your thinking for a short time will do. After allowing your thinking mind a short hiatus and entering this mild trance-like state, you will come back to your conscious, thinking body with fresh insight or a new approach to whatever you were working on.

The problem with thinking is that it gets in the way of receiving the intuited message. Obviously you don't want to stop thinking all the time, but when you try to figure out the solution, rather than letting the answer appear, you can come up with very different results.

I know you've had these experiences, however insignificant you think they are. You are thinking of a friend you haven't heard from for some time, and the phone rings — guess who? Someone keeps coming into your mind, and the next day at the supermarket, wham! You smack directly into that person in the checkout line.

You may think of this as coincidence, but I believe that there is more going on in these situations. You can call it synchronicity, coincidence, luck or chance. After having many, many of these experiences in my life, I can see that much more is going on here.

Over the past several years I have come to more fully understand some of the Native American traditions. I have been blessed by the opportunity to work with some of their teachers. Native Americans hold the feminine Spirit in highest regard. They teach that the Great Spirit or Creator gives women the ability to understand life's meaning through the intensity and pain of birth. They believe that men, on the other hand, learn only through circumstantial suffering. It is clear that the masculine and feminine essence each have their own destinies.

INTUITION IS SIMILAR TO DREAMING. We know that we dream, but we don't know how we dream. Intuitions are like knowing, but not knowing how we know it. My mother considered herself to be very intuitive; she was a big proponent of trusting her gut feelings. My three younger sisters and I grew up accepting that about her.

Because she was a superb cook and spent a lot of time in the kitchen, we nicknamed her the "kitchen witch." We spent many mornings around the kitchen table talking about the dreams we'd had the night before, and because my mother encouraged this we often shared elaborate details of our nocturnal meanderings. Each morning, the first thing she would ask my sisters and I was, "What did you dream last night?" We would share our dreams, she would tell us hers and, nodding or laughing, we would give each other confirmation. Whether crazy or very plausible, there was never any criticizing or poking fun at our dreams, so we learned to remember them and to share them in intricate detail. This exercise helped me develop trust in the messages that I receive. It has served me well throughout my life.

I thought it was commonplace to have vivid dreams, but was quite surprised later to find that many people do not remember their dreams. I remember several instances when my mother had intuitive feelings about things that proved to be correct — no matter how much we wanted to discredit her.

Since an intuitive nudge comes to us directly, without reason or logic, many distrust it as being irrational. But many enlightened women can remember a time when they had a feeling about someone, or something, that they ignored only to later regret it.

Most of the information we use in our daily lives is unconscious. In this way, we know much more than we realize. Just as we all have different learning styles — auditory, visual or kinesthetic — we can experience our intuition in different ways. Because much of our intuitive information comes through our senses (hearing, seeing, feeling or even smelling) when we learn to trust these senses they can become helpful tools in our personal and professional lives.

Just as exercising our bodies makes them stronger, we can exercise our intuition to make it stronger. The following list may trigger some ideas about how you can further trust your intuition.

When your heart is open, you are open to all of life. Intuition allows us to more fully experience ourselves.

10 *Keys to Feminine Intuition*

1. Acknowledge your feminine sexual essence
2. Know what you value
3. Develop a pure heart
4. Keep it open
5. Demonstrate kindness to all
6. Trust your heart to Spirit
7. Have faith in persistent messages
8. Envision a possible reality for a new world order
9. Act on those things that serve the highest purpose
10. Give thanks for all of it

We know when our kids are lying to us. They can tell us one thing, but everything else about what they are doing, rather than what they are saying, gives us other information about what is really going on. This is one level of knowing. We all have this wisdom. Our bodies tell us what's going on. "It's a gut feeling," we say. By the way, our kids know when we're lying to them, as well.

The physical body responds differently depending on what level of truth you are experiencing. Whether goosebumps or hard nipples, if your body has a physical reaction it is a pretty good indicator that you are reacting to something that you feel to be true. Breathe deeply. Go inside and connect with your Higher Self. Are you responding to something that is outside of yourself, or to something within?

Be clear about what is going on. Get feedback from other women (especially older, more experienced women) as to what you are feeling, seeing or sensing. Probe your reactions to what is going on. If the issue is in your relationship, no matter whose "fault," you may want to get the perspective of someone you know and trust.

When we are under stress we often become more rational, pushing our feelings and the messages from our intuition down even deeper. These messages, when suppressed over any length of time, can become actual symptoms of disease. Many stress-related illnesses, such as irritable bowel syndrome and gastritis, follow from suppressing our gut feelings. Working as a massage therapist and healer for more than 20 years, I saw how people's stress showed up in tight muscles, nervousness, upset stomachs and headaches. If the cause of the stress was not removed or shifted, these minor symptoms became exacerbated and resulted in a host of other disorders, ranging from chronic fatigue syndrome to depression.

Instead of ignoring these symptoms or medicating them away, I advised my clients to pay attention to what their bodies are trying to tell them. While in a deeply relaxed and meditative state, we spend time going inside, trying to remember what triggers the feelings, when they occur and what thoughts accompany the feelings.

Because all the information we have stored in our brain is related, there is synergy in intuitive retrieval. An automatic reflex triggers the right information without thinking. The more we function intuitively, the quicker the response. The more we rely on intuition, the more adept we become at recognizing the signals of intuition.

Depending on your individual learning style, you may find some ways of redeveloping your intuition more successful than others. This can be an intuitive exercise in itself. Try various approaches, and feel which ones work best for you. Trust your answers, then practice those things regularly. After a while, incorporate other techniques to further improve your proficiency.

You can really begin to have fun using your intuition. Some people say that intuition only works in crisis situations, or when tragic events happen. We know from experience that during these times intuition is very accessible. But that is like saying common sense is only available to us during times of emergencies. Intuition, like common sense, is available at all times if we are open and willing.

Musings & Blessings

WHAT PERSON HAS NOT AT SOME TIME HAD A STRONG FEELING about something, and then watched it come to pass? Often, we believe that they are just fleeting thoughts with no significance, and we let them go. But often when we trust ourselves, we understand that there has been a knowing of what was to come.

What happened the last time you didn't listen to your Spirit? What might have happened if you had paid heed to the messages you were given? When we put our trust in Spirit, we are listening to our Higher Selves.

Breathe in your truth with love and gratitude. Exhale. Breathe in love.

We need to be willing to let our intuition guide us,
and then be willing to follow that guidance fearlessly.
— SHAKTI GAWAIN —

The Gift of Kindness

My Darling Feminine Heart:

There are days when I forget
to show you the love and kindness
that you so deserve.
When I am kind to you
I am acknowledging the love
that I am.
The more kindness I show
to myself and to others,
the more peace I feel
in my mind and body,
and on the earth.
Thank you, dear Goddess,
for the sweet gift of kindness.

Unkindness is a spiritual disease.
— PARAMAHANSA YOGANANDA —

AT HER CORE, THE FEMININE HEART IS PURE SPIRIT. We are consciously aware of that, but we forget. We become distracted, and we let our feelings take over. Kindness is almost always seen as the exception these days, not the norm. Our local newspaper, like most, is filled with the usual stories of hate, fear and evil. However, the editors have started a small weekly section called "Acts of Kindness." On this page we can read stories of people helping others, not out of obligation but solely out of kindness. I guess kindness doesn't sell, though, because it only consists of a page or so, but at least it's a start.

When we engage in any unkind acts or feelings, we not only make ourselves miserable, but we actually damage our nervous systems. Also, we are not honoring that highest part within ourselves, the Goddess.

"I don't want to be a doormat," I hear women say when fighting fire with fire after being unkindly treated. But returning the fire does not serve anybody. Rather than behaving with anger, raising your voice and using harsh words, use your feminine wisdom to deflect the barbs being sent your way. Be like a flower — allow your heady perfume to disarm the assailant who is acting unjustly toward you. Use your wisdom in realizing that as a daughter of Infinite Intelligence you can bring light to even the most unsavory situations.

THE CONCEPT OF "PAYING IT FORWARD" means that when somebody does, says or gives you something with kindness, it is yours to pass on to the next person. This is not an obligatory pay-it-back situation, but a sincere passing on of the kindness that was given to you. You can give it to anybody, knowing that somebody, somewhere will benefit from your kind deed.

Several years ago my vivacious boss and I were getting on the elevator to go down for a snack. We had been having a good laugh about something, and the tears were rolling down our cheeks. As we entered the elevator, we acknowledged the dapper elderly gentleman already present.

"Good morning," we said simultaneously, smiling as the door closed behind us.

"Good morning," he answered politely, pulling himself up a bit. His small frame suddenly appeared younger as he pulled his shoulders back, exposing a rich red tie under his old-man overcoat.

"What a gorgeous tie!" I exclaimed. It was vintage fifties. I love the rich burgundy brocades of that era.

The old gentleman looked down and touched the rich sheen of the garnet-colored sateen fabric.

"I let my wife dress me this morning," he announced proudly.

We continued down, and out of the corner of my eye I saw him gracefully removing his hat from his shiny, wrinkled brow and gently placing it over his heart. I knew that his reverent action was a direct result of the kindness and sincerity that we had showed him. As a woman, I felt so honored and respected.

A silky mist filled my eyes. This man was responding to the true beauty and love that the divine feminine offers. We arrived at the main floor.

"Have a wonderful day," I said, turning around to watch him walk away.

"You too," he replied, waving his hand in a farewell gesture.

I saw a much younger man with a spring in his step heading toward the exit. He passed two more women that he must have acknowledged, because they had big smiles on their faces. I knew that he loved his wife from the way that he spoke, and that when he got home she would be the recipient of the kindness and respect we had shown him. This fortunate woman would then be able to share his kindness with others who passed through her life.

Kindness multiplies exponentially. The more kindness we extend to others, the quicker we will realize peace in our communities, and in our world.

Musings & Blessings

HOW OFTEN EACH DAY DO YOU MAKE A CONCERTED EFFORT to share the love and kindness that exists within? What is stopping you from sharing smiles of joy with others who so desperately need to have the light of your radiance guide them on their earthly journey?

Kindness is not just something you *do*, it is the quality of your *being* in what you *do*. Is what you do an act of kindness, or just an act?

Kindness is the language which the deaf can hear and the blind can see.
— MARK TWAIN —

The Gift of Listening

My Darling Feminine Heart:

I must apologize for rushing around so much
that I haven't heard your voice for some time.
Even when you scream out to me
I can hardly hear you
as I am not listening.
When I go into my heart
my ears actually hear
the sweet song of your message.
Thank you, Goddess, for giving me ears
that are connected to my heart.

The first duty of love is to listen.
— PAUL TILLICH —

ABY CRIES IN THE MIDDLE OF THE NIGHT, and his mother's eyes fly open. She listens intently for the nature of the cry. "Is he hungry, is he afraid, or has he wet his diaper?" she wonders. She continues to listen until she understands the message in his cry, and she responds accordingly.

A child comes home from school looking sullen. "How did things go today?" his mother asks. "It was okay," the child answers, but from the tone of his voice his mother knows to probe further. The Feminine Heart instinctively knows that much that is unsaid needs to be heard.

While shopping at the supermarket we run into the elderly lady who lives down the street. "Hello Mrs. Thompson, I haven't seen you for some time. How are things going?" we asked politely. We stand and listen patiently while our elderly neighbor talks about the new heart medication she is on; how her dog had to be put down, and how the cost of heating her poorly insulated home has skyrocketed. While she speaks, we listen with a loving and open Feminine Heart, nodding appropriately and adding encouraging remarks. What we may not know is that this is the first time anyone has shown interest in her life this week.

Later that day we finally get to see our partner and ask, almost routinely, "How was your day?" As he spouts off about how his manager handled a situation that affects his work performance we listen, sensing his frustration and anger. We offer a word of encouragement, perhaps rubbing his shoulders while acknowledging his feelings. These are not feelings that he shares with others at work, although inside he is bursting. When we listen with an open heart he feels loved, and that makes his situation at work seem less important.

That evening, the phone rings. It is a dear girlfriend. "Great to hear from you! How are things going?" we ask, again listening as she talks about the trouble she is having with her latest romantic pursuit. The man with whom she has shared her heart has done something to hurt her. In the tone of her voice we can feel her heart is starting to shut down. We continue to listen and empathize with her situation, because we've been in that place before. As the conversation ends her heart lightens, because she has shared her sadness and concern. She no longer feels alone. Once again, our love is able to support her. Whether she shares her loving and open heart with an uncaring man again will be her choice. What is important is that we've supported her in keeping her heart open.

Throughout our busy days we have many opportunities to speak with people, at work, at play, and in our homes. It is easy to have conversations with people without really listening. Giving our full attention, while sharing our love is truly one of the most-needed gifts of our time. A lot of conversation takes place throughout the day, yet the quality of listening during those conversations is often shallow.

I believe that the success of many of today's talk shows is due to the host's ability to listen. Thousands of people can tune into a talk show and listen to the problems and concerns of the guests. The most successful talk shows have hosts who have the gift of deep listening. Oprah is a master of listening. When we watch her interact with a guest, we feel listened to. It is as though she is in our family room with us, listening to our problems and concerns.

Listening is one of the most important gifts that the Feminine Heart has to offer. It is also the gift that we can give most often. When we are busy mentally checking off items on our to-do list, it is impossible to give open-hearted listening, no matter how deeply we look into our friend's eyes and nod appropriately. Often, we feel so needy to be heard that we can't wait to get our words in. We don't really listen. We interact in a series of interruptions, because we are so needy to be listened to.

The greatest listener is our Creator. When we sincerely share our thoughts, feelings and dreams with Spirit, we feel heard. In our deepest prayers, we feel deeply listened to. Once we feel deeply listened to, we are not so hungry to be heard. It is then that we truly have the capacity to listen to others. In our modern, fast-paced world the gift of listening is rare. Yet it is one of the most important. When you share the feminine gift of listening, not only are you being a good friend, you are being an angel, a bearer of light in the darkness.

Musings & Blessings

THERE IS A SAYING THAT GOD GAVE US ONE MOUTH AND TWO EARS so that we can listen twice as much as we talk. There is deep wisdom in this. When we stop talking, we hear much more than what is being said around us. When we foster a sense of quiet, we are actually listening with our hearts and not just our ears and our minds.

When you are with others, do you find yourself interrupting them? Or perhaps you like to finish other people's sentences for them. This is not only rude, it does not allow the other person to feel heard or honored.

Make a practice of listening more than you speak. Not only will your friends respond to you more readily, but what you do say will actually come from a deeper place than from the incessant chatter of your mind.

Have you ever tried not talking for a day? Many women would find this extremely difficult, but it is a worthwhile practice. When you have the opportunity to spend some time in solitude, give yourself the opportunity to remain silent. What you find may surprise you. Your heart's messages will actually be heard, as you have taken the time to listen.

If you want to be listened to, you should put time into listening.
– MARGE PIERCY –

The Gift of Mothering

My Darling Feminine Heart:

There is a part of me
that longs to pull the sorrows
of the world into my breast…
to soothe them with the tender
beating of my heart.
Whether my child or yours,
all living things are mine to cherish —
to care for and nurture.
First I must be my own divine mother
before I can truly mother
life in its totality.
With love in my heart
I know that when I serve
I am helping to heal
our great mother,
This place we call Mother Earth.
Thank you, Goddess, the great mother.

I am child of my mother, mother of my child.
I am a bridge between yesterday and tomorrow.
— INDIGO PANGEA —

THE ENLIGHTENED WOMAN SEES CONNECTION IN ALL OF LIFE. Nature, the world and the stars were your sisters as you slipped into this realm of physical reality. When the Feminine Heart is preparing to give birth, she must surrender to all of life and to all of death. Then divinity takes over. As you open up and let that deep love enter, you meet the force head on. The source of the creative power of all life must be allowed to enter you, pulling out the life force. This life force could be a child, a project or a dream.

Whenever we are manifesting something, we are in tune with the feminine flow. The great mother or Goddess is alive within, and we are going along for the ride. The ride of Spirit through life is unlike any other experience. We have a spiritual awakening when we connect with the creative force of the divine feminine spirit. From that place, we can offer the deep mothering that is so needed across our planet.

People around the world have adopted children from all over the planet. Dear friends rescued a one-year-old girl left on orphanage steps about six years ago. This was before Angelina and Brad made it a Hollywood thing to do. We all have the capacity to mother, as the mother archetype is universally expressed and needed.

Nothing soothes like a mother's nurturing sustenance. The nourishment of the mother is available on three levels: nurturing the body, nurturing the emotions, and nurturing the spirit. We can mother on all these levels, or on any one of them, and make a difference. Of course, the fuller the expression the more healing can take place.

You may give them your love but not your thoughts
For they have their own thoughts.
You may house their bodies, but not their souls,
For their souls dwell in the house of tomorrow, which
you cannot visit, not even in your dreams.
You may strive to be like them, but seek not to make them like you.
For life goes not backward nor tarries with yesterday.
You are the bows from which your children as living
arrows are sent forth.
– KAHLIL GIBRAN, *The Prophet* –

Musings & Blessings

HOW DEEPLY HAVE YOU ALLOWED YOUR FAMILY MEMBERS AND FRIENDS to feel mothered by you? I didn't say smothered, but mothered. Taking care of the place where the child in all of us craves to be nourished is a great undertaking.

The tenderness of the Feminine Heart cannot be matched in healing the wounded and the worn. Spirit grows exponentially when shared with the love and joy that a mother can offer. That place of peaceful beauty is a knowing that we never forget.

Try a little tenderness when dealing with any family members, as their hearts have already been battered. Be tender with your offering of food, with kisses planted on foreheads, with the words that you use to calm and reassure. Tenderness can soothe the most dispirited soul, reminding recipients that they too are love and loved. The mother love that we offer and share is filled with the love of the divine Mother.

Breathe in deeply. Feel the essence of your Feminine Heart. Exhale. Be … just be.

Nearly all of us receive our first lessons in peaceful living from our mothers, because the need for love lies at the very foundation of human existence.
– His Holiness the DALAI LAMA –

The Gift of Nurturing

My Darling Feminine Heart:

As much as my heart longs
to receive the love that is my birthright
I yearn to give of my heart as well.
My life passes needlessly empty
when I am not sharing
my heart, my love, my light.
I feel the need for nurturing
all around me.
Like baby birds with their beaks
outstretched to receive pieces
of expressed love.
My loving Spirit flies in to deliver
what they hunger for...
the sweet nurturing
of my Feminine Heart.
Thank you, Goddess, for nurturing me
so that I may nurture the hearts of others.

*Three basic needs — for food, security and love — are so mixed and mingled
and entwined that we cannot straightly think of one without the others.
So it happens that when I write of hunger, I am really writing about love
and the hunger for it, and warmth and the love of it and the hunger for it
... and then the warmth and richness and fine reality of hunger satisfied
... and it is all one.*
– M.F.K. Fisher –

CHEF MICHAEL SMITH, host of the weekly show *Chef at Large* on the Food Network Canada, comments on food and its potential to enrich our lives. "At heart, food is an inherently social experience. It's not just feeding your body, it's feeding your soul and your mind, and that's always been a communal thing, whether you call it cuisine or whether you just call it dinner."

It's a slow but burgeoning trend that the enlightened woman has come to acknowledge. How and what we feed our families is important. It is one of the highest acts of love and nurturing that we can do.

One of the most common mantras I hear from many of the harried women who make it to my workshops is: "You don't know how crazy my life is! By the time I leave work, I have to pick up the dry cleaning, take my son to soccer, answer phone calls and pick up something from the supermarket — and that's before I even start to think about preparing dinner."

Many people simply feel that there's not enough time in the day to get everything done, let alone stop at the local fresh food market to buy vegetables and fuss with a dinner that would make our mothers proud.

It's about priorities. It's more than how much time is spent in the preparation of food. It's about the spirit and intention behind how it is prepared and served. Simple food left in its natural state can be prepared easily and offered with great love.

A GROWING MOVEMENT IN OPPOSITION TO FAST-FOOD RESTAURANTS and mechanization within the food production industry began as a socio-political phenomenon in Italy. Called "Slow Food," this movement started in 1986 when McDonald's was planning to open a restaurant near the lovely Piazza di Spagna in Rome. Carlo Petrini, an Italian journalist distressed about the arrival of the golden arches near one of Rome's most beautiful public monuments, reacted by taking action. He organized a demonstration during which he and a group of friends brandished bowls of pasta as a public protest. This wave of protest created momentum all the way to Canada and back to Paris, France, where the international Slow Food organization was formed.

One of the declarations of this dedicated group was to restore the dining room table to its former glory as a place where friends and families gather to share stories about the day and about life in general. Intended to elevate the act of sharing food beyond the modern-day habit of quickly shoveling something down the gullet and moving on to the next activity, it was about the art of nurturing the people with whom we share our lives.

Several years ago in a *New York Times* interview, Slow Food founder Petrini explained his personal philosophy. "Breaking bread is an enrichment. Eating together and drinking together at the end of the day is a kind of friendship and communion, and when that doesn't exist it's a sadder, less-cohesive society," he lamented.

Recent studies conducted at both Harvard and Columbia universities suggest that by not eating together, today's frantically rushed families are contributing to a wide range of social issues including childhood obesity, teen drug abuse, poor grades and even household stress.

As enlightened women, we are aware that most of the time responsibility for bringing the family together at mealtime falls on our shoulders. Many women are feeling tapped out by their never-ending list of responsibilities. But someone has to do it.

In her book, *The Surprising Power of Family Meals*, author Miriam Weinstein suggests, "We have managed to convince ourselves that hanging out in the kitchen for an hour with our kids, siblings or parents — chopping, eating, cleaning up, all accompanied by the ebb and flow of daily chatter — is demeaning, embarrassing, not worth our time."

Weinstein says that it is because we have lost other, stronger communal bonds that the family meal has become so important. It is one of the few habits that has not disappeared from memory.

Unfortunately, many of our children are brought up in cities without access to gardens and farms, and they have never experienced first-hand the source of their food. Their sensibilities about food, the preservation of what real food tastes like, and honoring the cycles of the earth that produce our food, have been lost to them. As a consequence, it is very difficult for them to pass on a sense of reverence for these cycles to their children (see The Gift of Heritage).

Several years ago when my son was small I often assisted at his school during the lunch hour, helping the kids open their lunches. Almost all the lunches came out of plastic packaging. I noticed that many lunches consisted of processed cheese with hard little floury sticks that were used to poke into the "cheese." I saw lots of expensive packaging, with not a whole lot of food value inside the packaging.

My goal isn't to slam the food producers of the world although sure, their lunches could have been more nutritious. What alarmed me was what was missing in these children's food — the love and nurturing. When an edible oil product disguised as cheese is piped into plastic containers there is little value for our children. No human hand had made these lunches. Many children today are growing up in homes where the feminine aspects of nurturing, healing and intimacy are not available. Their mothers are so busy pursuing masculine-oriented goals that they do not have time to make nutritious lunches. Their children do not receive the energetic goodness of the nurturing that comes from food prepared with care by the person who loves them more than anyone on this planet.

F OOD, LIKE ALL LIVING THINGS, CARRIES ITS OWN VIBRATION. *Like Water for Chocolate*, a wonderful novel by author Laura Esquivel, describes this perfectly. In her story, a woman overcome by sadness and grief resulting from a broken heart is cooking a meal to be served at a huge wedding banquet. Her deep sadness produces tears that fall into the pot she is tending. These tears filled with resentment, sadness and fear are energetically stirred into the ingredients and later fed to the wedding guests. After the celebration is over, everyone who has tasted her food falls ill.

This makes for an interesting story, but it also poignantly shows how energy can be transferred into the food we prepare.

Research shows that most women who work outside of the home are also responsible for the feeding of their families. If time is of the essence, don't worry as much about *what* you prepare as *how* you prepare it. A simple sandwich made with a loving and nurturing intention nourishes your child's body and satisfies his or her emotional and spiritual needs on a deeper level as well. This takes no more time, money or energy. It is the intention in your heart as you prepare the food that makes a difference to the people who are eating it.

This is one of the best reasons to give thanks for our food before eating it. The intention of gratitude changes the way that our Spirit receives the food. As enlightened women, we know that our bodies, mind and Spirit are inextricably connected. We cannot affect one aspect of the whole without affecting each of the parts.

Food, like all living things, carries its own vibration.

Although most people today don't have the space or inclination to grow their own food, many places exist where we can get much closer to the source of our food. Taking our kids to the local farmer's market, or to farms where they can pick their own produce, connects them to real food grown in soil. A carrot that has a little bit of earth left on it has such a different flavor than the carrots found in the frozen food department of the local supermarket.

Ask your child to tell you about eggs and milk. See how much understanding there is of the whole food chain. Where can you make a difference in the experience your loved ones have with the food they eat?

As a busy woman with a full schedule, this may sound like another make-work project for you to fit into your already over-filled life. Engaging your family in food preparation in your home may seem like more hassle than it's worth. You know the mess, the instruction and all the extra persuasion it will take to get them involved, especially when the children are young. It may seem like extra work, and indeed it may be. So scale down on your need to have everything perfect. A child who has helped to prepare sandwiches or celery stuffed with almond butter will probably enjoy the food just as much, if not more, for having contributed to the meal and having shared time with you.

I started delegating food preparation with my son at a very early age, just as my mother had done with me. Yes, in the beginning it takes twice as long to get half as much done, but the investment has become time well spent. Now he often shows up in the kitchen to help prepare a meal — usually pastas of some kind, but he is always so proud of his achievement. I will usually have some fresh vegetables to serve as an accompaniment, but everyone gets a break and he now realizes how much effort goes into the preparation of a good meal.

Giving thanks at mealtime always makes a meal more special, no matter how humble the menu.

Having shared our home with various students from different countries, we have come to learn the different customs of giving thanks for the food we eat. Of all the things that we do as a family, I believe that giving thanks is the most important. It helps create our food experience.

Besides eating dinner together, this is the time when we can discuss the day we've had. Sometimes it is the only time we come together to find out what is happening in each other's lives — it's an opportunity to share our challenges and accomplishments. Sometimes it is almost like having a therapy session over dinner. In my experience, dinner is the only meal where these things can be shared — breakfast is often rushed and we are all off doing our own things at lunch.

It doesn't always work that we share dinner together. Yes, like all families we have other commitments, classes and engagements. I try to keep these to a minimum, however, and often say *no* to things that aren't important.

Of course, many of us would rather do other things than spend the day cooking in the kitchen. The use of slow cookers and clay bakers can help immensely. You can start slow cooking vegetables or meat in the morning and come back from the day's activities to the delicious aroma of a home-cooked meal.

Again, what you cook is not as important as your intention when you put the food together. Do you serve a meal to your family with a sense of frustration or resentment? The enlightened woman is aware of the mood she is in when preparing a meal for herself and her family.

Try cooking with love. See if it not only lowers your heart rate, but opens your family's hearts with the love and gratitude of having food that feeds their souls as well as their bodies.

When thinking about preparing a meal, start with a deep breath. Bring love and a sense of gratitude into your heart. Then thoughtfully and slowly assemble the ingredients you have on hand. With intention, handle each ingredient consciously. Give thanks for its contribution to your family's needs. Continue to prepare your meal with a song in your heart, rather than focusing on your day's trouble or any resentment you may have. Now is the time to concentrate on maximizing the goodness that is present in the food. Your family will receive the benefits and love you for it. You will have the knowledge that you are giving so much more than filling the tummies of your loved ones.

MANY WOMEN TODAY ARE RESPONSIBLE FOR NURTURING AND CARING for our spouses and offspring. Many of us also have another responsibility. In our aging society, many women are confronted with the care and nurturing of dying friends and family members. We offer so much to our loved ones as they move toward the end of their lives. Find ways to bring peace and feelings of love to those who are preparing to leave their physical bodies. Usually the simplest expressions of love are the most appreciated.

My lovely friend Carleen shared this story about how she helped nurture her grandmother when she was preparing to pass from this world.

"I have always been very close with my maternal grandmother. She was a sweet woman and taught me many things that are special to me. Just before I went to what was to be our last visit in the hospital, I picked a lovely bouquet of colorful, fragrant sweet peas. She just beamed when I handed her the flowers. With both hands she put those flowers to her nose and inhaled deeply. She smiled and seemed to be in ecstasy. She died within the hour. I know that she left this planet with joy in her heart, and that her final moments were filled with things that she held precious. I felt like I made a real difference in her transition over to the other side."

Whether we are nurturing the living or the dying matters not. What is most important is that we allow ourselves to express that gift often, wherever we can.

Musings & Blessings

WITH THE LITTLE TIME THAT WE HAVE, how can we put more love into the food we prepare for our loved ones? It doesn't matter how simple the food we prepare. The important thing to be aware of is the intention with which we prepare it.

Do you grudgingly prepare sandwiches for your children at the end of a harried day? Become present to what you are doing, and spread a layer of love and light between the peanut butter and jam. Where is your attention while you prepare and offer the food that sustains your family's bodies, minds and spirits?

Breathe in love as you prepare food for loved ones ... exhaling that love into your soon-to-be-eaten meal.

A good cook is like a sorceress who dispenses happiness.
— ELSA SCHIAPARELLI —

The Gift of Radiance

My Darling Feminine Heart:

When I stumble through life
I look at the ground
fearful of getting hurt further.
When I shine
full of love
Goddess smiles gently,
blessing everyone.
The world is blessed by my radiance.
I allow it to shine brightly
lighting a path for others
to follow through the darkness.
Thank you, Goddess,
for the sparkling gift of radiance.

*I don't believe makeup and the right hairstyle alone can make a woman beautiful.
The most radiant woman in the room is the one full of life and experience.*
— SHARON STONE —

FEMININE SEXUAL RADIANCE — nothing on earth is more powerful than that. With infinite intelligence our Creator ensured that this would preserve our species.

Marketers know this. While watching television or reading a magazine, do you ever see advertisements calling out: "buy this product for duller hair," or "for that gray look use this product." No, it is always about glossy lips, shining hair or that radiant glow. Many women spend more time and money to have sparkling eyes, brilliant teeth, shiny hair and radiant skin, than they do on enriching their hearts and minds.

It is always about radiance. The masculine is attracted to the most radiant thing in the room. Unfortunately, sometimes that is a television or computer screen.

If you're schlepping around with a closed heart, just waiting for him to notice you and give you some of his time, he may not even see you. I hear women complain about this all the time. "I just want to talk to him" or "I just want to have some communication, to connect. He wants to watch the football game or play on the computer."

More than whatever it is you are radiating, the flicker of the television has his attention. I'm not saying that you should walk around in shiny spandex — it's not about that. The feminine radiance I'm talking about comes from within and it shines out through your eyes, from your spirit of love.

A femininely radiant woman is an attractive woman. When we don't express our love and let our hearts shine, the masculine doesn't experience our radiant feminine sexual essence. Although he may see his woman, he is not moved to reach out and take her hand or embrace her heart. He may bypass his woman as he reaches for the remote control. I have heard this complaint far too often from women, and have felt the perceived betrayal myself. How do you compete with a television? You don't. You can only be your divine radiant self and attract his attention in a way that serves you both.

Feminine radiance is love. It is the expression and outpouring of love from that limitless fountain that is all of life. When we don't express the love that lies latent in our hearts, we are denying not only ourselves, but others as well, of the gifts that only the Feminine Heart can give. The most powerful form of attraction is the radiance of God's light shining out from our eyes.

The desire to be attractive and noticed is a natural part of feminine sexual essence. However, many women interpret that desire as the need to show more skin and private parts than is actually necessary. What the Feminine Heart desires on a deeper level, is to be seen as the manifestation of the divine that she is. We want the Goddess that resides within to be acknowledged. We deeply desire to be seen as the love that we are.

The radiance of the Feminine Heart comes from deep within our soul. It is brought out into the world through the radiant light of love in our eyes. Wherever we look, we have the opportunity to share the limitless love that resides within.

Radiance is not about physical beauty. Radiance is a spiritual quality, not a physical attribute. It has nothing to do with age, clothing or the sparkle of gems. Not everyone is physically beautiful, but every woman can be spiritually radiant. Radiance is the quality which attracts and inspires. When we allow our hearts to open to that divine connection with Spirit we invite in the beauty and radiance of the angels. Even the most physically beautiful woman will age and her youthful beauty will diminish with time. Spending time and energy developing your inner beauty is a worthwhile endeavor. The timeless beauty of an open heart and a radiant Spirit will never fade, no matter how many decades you grace this earth.

Next time you are in a room full of people, watch who radiates the brightest. We are born radiant, full of life, love and possibility. Over time, the harsh unrealities of the world send us messages that we are not love, that we are not Spirit, that we are not children of God.

It is easier for a young woman to radiate love because she hasn't had the weight of the world cast a veil over her inner light. Perhaps her feminine essence hasn't been squelched yet because she hasn't had to protect her Feminine Heart. The need to protect herself, to take care of herself, to support herself, to look after sick kids or to spend years in an unfulfilling job hasn't yet taken its toll. Perhaps she is a neophyte in the arena of heartache, betrayal and rejection. Life's responsibilities, hardships and heartbreaks haven't knocked the radiance out of her … yet.

But what is more powerful, more compelling and deeper than the radiance of a young woman, is the radiant glow emitted by a mature woman who knows her true nature. Conscious of her wisdom and grace, she knows the worth of her soul and the beauty of her inner truth. Most women don't get to that point of understanding unless they've had some life experience to go along with it.

If you want to turn up the volume on the radiance meter, remember that it's not about having the trendiest clothes or showing the most cleavage. Because the masculine tends to be visual, you will get some attention physically, but the masculine heart won't be compelled to connect with you. Unfortunately, that's what the feminine wants — to connect at the heart level. We don't just want our bodies to be stimulated, we want our hearts and spirits to be embraced as well. The most common yearning I heard from women while working as a professional matchmaker, was that they craved a deeper, more heartfelt connection with their intimate partner.

The next time you are grocery shopping and you see a young child or baby in a cart, as you pass by project energy out to them. See what happens. Because young children haven't yet closed down their hearts, they will receive you and light up. Perhaps they will smile, or reach out to you. If you really make an effort to communicate your unconditional love, they may

The most common yearning I heard from women while working as a professional matchmaker, was that they craved a deeper, more heartfelt connection with their intimate partner.

actually start to laugh. Or they may want to pull themselves out of the shopping cart just so they can get closer to your uncensored, innocent smile.

Even people who have been closed down for years, with layer after layer of cladding protecting their hearts, can still get a sense of the gift you have just given them. They can still pick up on your pure and open heart.

WARS HAVE STARTED AND MEN HAVE DIED for the honor of having a radiant woman be part of their lives. The most attractive woman in the room is the woman who radiates love, grace and beauty from her Feminine Heart. A grown man will be awed in the presence of a radiant woman. Her presence is a blessing in his life, bringing him closer to his heart while she opens herself up as the source of love and life. A man is blessed by the presence of the healing energy of an open and loving heart. Like a moth to a flame, your light gives the masculine drive to accomplish his purpose. If his purpose is worthwhile, give of your light generously.

If we let the worries and cares of the world weigh down our hearts too heavily, they start to ache. Slowly but surely, the light of the heart is dimmed. Before you know it, you are a dim bulb. Perhaps your light is almost snuffed out. You know that you are going down.

One of the easiest ways to re-ignite your heart's flame is to go to a quiet spot and go inside your heart, in prayer or meditation. Sitting quietly, feel the love that you are. Breathing deeply, feel the presence of Spirit with you and give thanks. In that place of peace and gratitude, breathe in all the love around you. Just breathe in love … .

Another way to increase your radiance is to celebrate life. Laugh, love, sing and dance until your heart is filled with joy. Give thanks for all the love that you have and all the love that you are. Feel the presence of Spirit move through you. Are you glowing yet?

Be like a sparkling diamond. Gift the world with your bright light of love. Every day find ways to share yourself with others. Materially, physically, mentally and spiritually — there are many ways you can awaken another soul to experience the abundance of the love of God, the source of all life.

"The sun shines equally on a piece of charcoal and a diamond placed side by side in the sunlight, but the diamond reflects the light while the charcoal does not," says Paramahansa Yogananda in *Journey to Self-Realization*.

Musings & Blessings

DO YOU FIND YOURSELF BEING STINGY WITH YOUR RADIANCE, saving it only for special people or special occasions? Let your love shine. If you are not sharing all you have and all that you are, you are not living your full potential as the daughter of Goddess. When you remember who you are, love will once again be present in your eyes.

Breathe in the love and bright healing light that you are. Exhale any darkness. Breathe in love.

What … is a miracle?
Nothing more or less than this: a highly illumined soul,
one who has brought his life into harmony with the higher spiritual laws.
– RALPH W. TRINE –

The Gift of Relationships

My Darling Feminine Heart:

I welcome you to join with me.
Do not be afraid.
I want nothing from you
that does not heal each of our hearts.
In return what I will give you
is a reflection of yourself.
In that reflection
I give you everything.
Thank you, Goddess
for all healing relationships.

The people we are in a relationship with are always a mirror,
reflecting our own beliefs, and simultaneously we are mirrors reflecting their beliefs.
So relationship is one of the most powerful tools for growth …
if we look honestly at our relationships,
we can see so much about how we have created them.
— Shakti Gawain —

Nothing affects the Feminine Heart's well-being more than the quality of her personal relationships. If her closest relationships are suffering, she brings that pain to all areas of her life. The boundaries between home, work and personal life are less-defined for the Feminine Heart. Life is an interlacing vine of love and gratitude.

The Feminine Heart yearns for a trustworthy man who has a purpose and a mission that she can support — something she feels strongly about. I laughed when I heard Marianne Williamson say, "If a train doesn't stop at your station, it's not your train." Don't spend time looking for a man. Let the masculine come and find you. Does the rose know its beauty by picking itself, or by allowing the beauty to be picked by another?

As a professional matchmaker, it always amazed me that people are in a state of one of the following: looking to get into a new relationship, looking to improve a current love situation, or trying to get out of a relationship that no longer serves. Relationships, like life, are not static. They are always changing and evolving.

The quality and the state of our relationships affect us profoundly. We cannot visually see what is happening to our bodies while we are under the dark veil of a relationship gone sideways — one where we no longer love, honor or respect the other. Research has shown that even having negative thoughts about your partner can affect their vitality and "suck them dry." Once you become aware of the power of your thoughts, the responsibility of living an authentic, integral and intentional life becomes mandatory. You can no longer blame anyone else for your life situation.

Carolyn Myss, PhD, talks about "woundology" in her book *Why People Don't Heal and How They Can*. This is a phrase that she coined to express the kinship we feel with people who've shared our suffering, our pain and our wounds.

"People also use woundology to make powerful romantic connections," states Myss. "Many people describe their "soul mate" as the person they have finally found who understands the emotional pain they had experienced as children. Such a bond can certainly feel romantic in the early states of a relationship, but its foundation is actually injury, pain and fear. The partnership is inevitably threatened when one of them decides the time has come to release the past and move on."

That is why group therapy has been useful over several decades. Programs such as the 12-step program are so helpful in establishing a community for people to share and experience the unity of one.

IF YOU WANT TO ATTRACT A PERFECT PARTNER, you must ask yourself, "Who must I be to attract a partner who is perfect for me?" There are lots of potential partners out there. Once you set your intention, the person you want to attract will come onto your radar screen, no matter where the person is now. The clearer you are about who you are and what you stand for, the sooner the right partner will be honing in on you.

My mother used to say that there is no such thing as a perfect man. I believe any man that we attract on a deep level is perfect for us as a mirror for our own learning. *Who must I be to attract a partner who is perfect for me?* You don't have to date him or marry him, but for some reason you have attracted this person into your world. The perfection is that you are perfect in who you are being, and he is the perfect mirror for you and your learning. For some reason he has been pulled in by your force of feminine radiance. If nothing else, you can just ask yourself, "Who am I being that has attracted this person into my energy field?"

We may not always want some of these people around. As women, one of the gifts we have been given is intuition. Trust your Higher Self to know if this person has come into your life for your highest purpose. It is a deep desire of the Feminine Heart to be attractive and noticed for her feminine essence. But don't be mislead by the headiness of having a man attracted to you. Flattering as it may be, he may not be deserving of your time or energy.

Relationships are sacred and we must treat them as such. Whether it is an intimate relationship or one with a friend, colleague or neighbor, it is important that we offer the best of what we have to further the possibility of peace in our homes, offices and communities.

Gerard Grant, a dear friend and mentor, gave me an analogy regarding trust in relationships that I have shared with many others. Gerard passed on several years ago, but I still feel his presence and guidance. He said that when two people meet and connect at the soul level, the quality of the relationship is like a precious thread of gold. The tensile strength of pure gold is very strong, and can take an extreme amount of pressure without breaking. If, however, the pull becomes so great that the thread does break, it can never be repaired to its original strength. One may tie several knots in an attempt to rejoin the threads, but no matter how many knots are tied, the golden thread will never be as strong as it was before it was broken.

Trust takes time to build, but only a moment to be broken.

THE MOST COMMON COMPLAINT I HEAR ABOUT MEN from women is that they don't feel emotionally connected with their intimate partners. Often their masculine partners are more concerned with a genital connection than with a heart connection, or they are stuck in their minds.

You can, in your wisdom, support a man in shifting his energy from his mind, into his body so that he can feel his heart. This is one of the gifts that you offer the masculine. Your Feminine Heart can help to heal and open his heart. As he becomes stronger and more present in what he has to offer as a man, you will get that back. Don't be stingy about it. Open up your heart, and let the sun shine in.

Of course, this is not always easy. We do it because our love's depth does not depend on what we want. It is about them — their well-being, their safety, their sense of being loved. Pleasing and satisfying our partner is not about giving up to another, but about authentically following our birthright — the giving of love. Spirit exists to give and not to take. Because receiving is the other side of this coin, it is also mandatory that we open our Feminine Hearts up wide, receiving all love that will come back to us, without our need for it. When you see yourself as a Goddess of giving, all your relationships will become sacred.

Musings & Blessings

IF YOU ARE INTERESTED IN HAVING A GREAT RELATIONSHIP with another person, how much effort have you put in to having a great relationship with yourself? First look at the relationship you have with your Creator. No matter how wonderful a person is, that person cannot fulfill you if you are not filled with the love of Spirit. Breathe in the love for all life. Exhale pain and suffering. Breathe in love.

The relationship we have with ourselves will be reflected in our relationships with others. Do you spend quality time giving yourself what your heart desires, or do you expect another person to fulfill those needs? When you have a deep relationship with the Goddess within, all your relationships will be blessed.

If it's your time, love will track you down like a cruise missile.
– LYNDA BARRY –

The Gift of Romance

My Darling Feminine Heart:

I long for those tender whispers
that catch the lobe of my ear en route to my heart.
Your words of love sustain me and
remind me of my radiant beauty.
My body swoons when I feel the honor and respect
that you bestow upon me.
I surrender my heart.
You have captured it with your love …
because you insist that I fly alongside the angels.
Thank you, Goddess, for loving me as I truly am.

God brings us love, but we must meet it with courage or it will slip through our hands.
When love walks in, we had best meet it with backbone.
— MARIANNE WILLIAMSON —

I HAVE YET TO MEET A WOMAN WHO DOESN'T CRAVE MORE romance in her life. How many times have we waited, pining for and fantasizing about a man who we dreamed would be our prince? The enlightened woman dreams about a man who not only loves what he sees, but all that he doesn't see as well. We want to be seen at our core. Many men don't get past our exteriors because we don't give them a chance. We shut down our hearts because he is too tall, too short, too hairy, not hairy enough, too quiet, too talkative, too smart, not smart enough, too….

As a professional matchmaker, I heard all the reasons why women reject men and the possibility of romance and love. It is no wonder that some men regard the whole idea of romance as not worth the effort.

I once heard a story about a male moose that wandered onto a farm in Vermont and fell in lust with a Hereford cow. Despite his continual nuzzling, she resisted his animal charms and refused to mate. This determined moose hung around for two and a half months until his antlers fell off, his libido dropped and he finally got the message.

We chuckle as we can relate this story to human interactions. Putting emotional energy into a romantic overture with someone who doesn't see our light is a waste of time and energy. Besides the possibility that it could trigger a major carbohydrate binge, it can actually do a great deal of damage to our sense of self.

In the last couple of years there has been a proliferation of books written about the misery of unrequited love. A couple of best-selling books were written by men for women. *He's Just Not That Into You*, by Greg Behrendt and Liz Tuccillo, and *Be Honest: You're Just Not That Into Him Either*, by Ian Kerner, explain some of the aspects of the miseries that women face when they can't find a suitable mate who will commit to them. These authors sense the loss of self-love that women feel when they are unloved. They give advice on how to deal with the "brutes."

The enlightened woman is not distraught when a man who has captured her attention does not return her affections. After all, she has an intimate relationship with her beloved, her Higher Self, that never disappoints. She knows that she is not alone. Finding a romantic partner is the icing on the cake. It brings down to earth the heavenly delight that we experience with the One. It makes it real. When Spirit is involved in your romantic connections, you can hear the whole choir of angels singing the Hallelujah Chorus.

Marianne Williamson, in her wonderful book *Enchanted Love*, says, "We have not put romance and sex in the same category as God and Spiritual practice for a very long time, if ever. But it is time for our generation of Westerners to claim for ourselves, in the context of our own traditions, the notion of holy romance in today's astounding world."

My clients often voiced disappointment in their experience of romance. Many women and some men have had the experience of connecting on the physical and emotional levels, but they yearned for something more...more heartfelt connections and meetings of Spirit in their romantic interludes. While romance may have been present, the deep romantic connection where the Spirit of each partner is felt and shared, was missing. Often, women blame men for their inability to open their hearts enough to share on a deep level. But we must take responsibility for the men we have attracted into our lives — we always attract partners who are mirrors of our own souls. There is no one to *— we always attract partners who are mirrors of our own souls.* blame. There is only our ability to surrender our hearts to God. God is love. Then, and only then, are we available for that divine romance that we all crave.

As Deepak Chopra says, "The only difference between romance and relationship, spiritually speaking, has to do with surrender. Surrender has to become a conscious goal — it is no longer a given. As such, it can bring the same joy and delight as falling in love, the same sense of play that releases new lovers from their ego burdens."

There are plenty of guys around who will sleep with a woman who has a beautiful shell, but they aren't interested in hanging around for long if her heart is closed. If a guy is so desperate that he will marry a beautiful woman with a hardened heart he will ultimately pay, big-time, either in the loneliness in his heart, or in the battering of his self-esteem.

I believe that we attract people who match our pattern of what we need to learn or experience. If you took responsibility for the man that you've attracted into your life, there would be no reason to slam or mock the man. You chose him.

One of the most desirable qualities women look for in men is that they be honest and trustworthy. Without spending time with a man in various situations, it is difficult to assess these qualities, especially when we are attracted by other, more obvious attributes. But there are things you can look for and things you can ask that will help you to decipher fairly quickly if a man is deserving of your time and energy.

One of the quickest indicators of a good man is to look at his actions. How does he treat people? Does he show others kindness and respect? If you are out for a meal is he courteous to the waiter, or to other people who are in service to him? You can tell a great deal about a man by the way he treats people who are less fortunate than he is, or who have nothing to offer him.

Is he present when he is talking to you, or are his eyes flitting to every little skirt walking by? Is he grounded? What is he up to in his life? Does he know his purpose? When a man is clear about his purpose, you can decide if what he is doing with his life is worthy of your presence, your energy and your heart. Be clear about what lights up your heart, and don't settle for less.

When you are with him, do you feel as though you are the most important thing in that moment? Or is he only giving you a tidbit of himself? Don't settle for crumbs. Out of neediness and loneliness, sometimes a woman will offer her mind and her body to a man who not only does not deserve her, but who will actually harm her.

To fully surrender your Feminine Heart to a man you must know where your man is headed…his purpose. Then you can feel in your heart if you want to support or accompany him. If you are considering a sexual relationship with a man, the stakes become much higher than just sharing a meal or going for a walk with him. When we share ourselves sexually with a man, we take on his energy. That stays with us long after the sexual sharing. Be selective.

The Feminine Heart knows at her deepest core when she is being served by a man she has chosen — and unless she has been raped, she gets to choose. Remember, you are in the driver's seat when it comes to having sexual relationships. You get to choose. Be choosey. You owe it to yourself, and the next deserving man who comes along will be blessed by your selectivity.

If you are attracted to a man but unsure of your feelings for him, you can ask for feedback from a few of your girlfriends whose opinions you respect; girlfriends who know you and love you.

Have a dinner party with a few of your trusted girlfriends and introduce the man who is potentially deserving of your love and affection. Ask your friends (at a later date) their honest opinions, and be open to feedback. You may not like what you hear. Or it may trigger something that you had already thought about, or something that you will notice yourself at some time in the future.

Don't judge what your friends tell you. Allow them to feel safe in saying what comes up for them. They know your history and patterns with men, and your relationships from the past. They will be looking at this man through their own filters, but their knowing of you will be more objective than your romantic hopes and dreams. This requires trust, honesty and respect on both sides, from all parties involved.

Don't judge their answers as positive and negative. This is just extra information. See whether it concurs with your intuitive feelings or not. If you go to your new beau, or to your existing partner, and say, "Janet told me that she thinks you're too critical of me," this lays blame, and this defeats the whole purpose of the Feminine Heart.

If you want a romantic partner, the first thing you must be clear about are your own values. What's important to you? In the matchmaking business, we match on values. People's values don't have to be exactly the same, but it's useful if they are complementary in three areas. How do you like to spend your time? How do you like to spend your money? What kinds of people do you like to associate with? When they are not similar, these three areas create more problems down the road in relationships than almost anything else.

People would always come to me with a list of "desired" qualities. You know the list. You've probably written it yourself, even if just in your mind. It usually looks something like this: honest, attractive, fun, successful, good sense of humor, adventurous etc, etc. etc. After listening patiently to these lists, I would always ask, "Why would this person want to date you? Do you possess all the qualities that you are seeking in a potential romantic partner?"

Often my client would look at me, uncertain about what she or he had to offer. I would explain that we must be the partner we would like to have. If you want a partner who has certain characteristics, you must possess those qualities yourself for that kind of person to be attracted to you. If kindness is a quality that you value in a person, don't expect to attract a kind partner if you are mean-spirited. You must be the kind of person you want to attract into your life.

> *You must be the kind of person you want to attract into your life.*

Musings & Blessings

WHAT DO YOU DO TO BRING MORE ROMANCE INTO YOUR LIFE? If romance is something you desire, are you waiting for the perfect partner to give it to you, or are you willing to give yourself what you deeply desire? When we take actions to give ourselves what we want, we are sending a message out to the universe that we believe we deserve it. Buy yourself flowers, or a book of poetry, if that calls out to the romantic aspect of your Feminine Heart. You cannot expect another person to give you something that you are not willing to give yourself. Breathe in love.

To love oneself is the beginning of a life-long romance.
— OSCAR WILDE —

The Gift of Sensuality

My Darling Feminine Heart:

When my back arches a certain way
I feel a deep yearning to get closer to you.
Preparing myself for that next wave of bliss
I move my body to flow
with the gift of love.
You feel my longing and you are moved.
As I express my physical delights
you smile, knowing I am loving being in the now.
Thank you, Goddess, for the sensual gifts of life.

*Sensuousness, which encompasses the whole range of physical delight,
is often considered low compared to the heights the soul can reach.
But spirituality must also be sensuous,
because a spiritual person is one who lives fully in the present moment,
which means living fully in the body.*
— DEEPAK CHOPRA —

SEX HAS BECOME SO BLASÉ IN OUR SOCIETY that sensuality is almost passed over. The nuances of sensuality aren't nearly as obvious as those of sex, yet given as a gift of the Feminine Heart, sensuous offerings can delight, nurture and heal both the observer and the giver.

Many women today don't feel that they have enough time to share this aspect of themselves, as it is not an instant fix. It takes time to entice the juice of life into our daily activities, turning everyday events into offerings of sensuality. Some women don't know how to embrace that aspect of their femininity. We may be born with the gift, but if we've never opened it we don't even know what lies inside.

Jean Shinoda Bolen says, "Every woman who falls in love with someone who is also in love with her is at that moment a personification of the Aphrodite archetype. Transformed temporarily from an ordinary mortal into a goddess of love, she feels attractive and sensual, an archetypal lover."

IN MANY CULTURES, sensuality is not only revered as a tool for healing, but as a tool that actually evokes the spirit of man to be more fully present. The temple-dancing girls of India, for example, performed for only the most spiritually evolved men of intelligence and respect in the community. Their beauty, femininity and grace were a blessing to these men, many of whom had renounced sex as a way of staying more focused on their spiritual path … a blessing indeed! These young women were highly trained from childhood. Every move, every sashay, was used to evoke a feeling, a thought or just a sensation of pure delight. The intention was to create a strong polarity with the masculine by offering one of the most delightful aspects of the Feminine Heart, the gift of sensuality.

This magical gift, if offered reverently with an open heart, can actually transform the most hard-assed, hotwired, angry man into a purring little kitty. Many ancient traditions understood the power of sensuality to heal and inspire, and selected specific young women to educate them in the art. Sensuality is a gift that can be offered with grace and wisdom.

When the gift is offered, most people with a strong masculine essence will respond physically at first. However, it can be used as a tool to open a man's heart. In your infinite wisdom you can take him deeper into his heart than he could ever manage on his own. Offer him your beautiful, radiant energy charged with the fullness of light and love. Sensuality is a healing and delightful gift. This is a much deeper offering than just contributing to his erection.

Good work. Helping to lift the vibration on this planet isn't an easy job, but it is the most important job you will ever have. Our men, children, animals — every living organism — can benefit from our gifts. Sharing our sensuality is like the sweet icing dripping down the side of the cake. It's that extra little gift that makes us feel alive, juicier and more of who we came here to be.

Musings & Blessings

How often and to whom do you offer your gifts? Do you save the gift of sensuality only for a special someone, or do you give your gifts to the world? When you pour that cup of hot steaming tea for a friend, do you do it with the grace that you would bestow upon your beloved? Why not? Is your friend not a child of God? Gift your friend with your gracious sensuality and hear the bells of her heart chime. All of life responds to the beauty of the sensual gifts offered in love.

Breathe in. Feel the air as it flows through your nasal passages, filling your lungs with love and light — you sensual creature, you! Exhale, relaxing any sense of tightness or physical constriction. Breathe in love.

Sensuality soars when my body sings to my heart's song.
— Beverly Ann Monsebroten —

The Gift of Service

My Darling Feminine Heart:

I have so much to give
that would serve others in many ways.
When my heart is open in love
everyone who passes my way
receives something from my soul.
This is my privilege.
I will not shirk my greatest offerings…
Mother earth's evolution depends on it.
Thank you, Goddess, for using me up in service.

Service is the rent we pay for the privilege of living on this earth.
— SHIRLEY CHISHOLM —

TO BE IN SERVICE IS PART OF OUR NATURAL BIRTHRIGHT. It is through our contributions to others that we serve ourselves by further opening our hearts and our capacity to give and receive love.

From an early age we are taught to be in service to the people we love — our spouses, our children, our friends and neighbors. Many women spend much of their days giving to others. If this service comes out of a sense of duty or obligation, however, the result is very different than if we serve with love and a sense of joy.

When we feel that it is our duty to be in service to others we go through the motions, with our hearts not fully engaged. Sure things get done, but not with the beauty and grace that the Feminine Heart expresses so naturally. The energy shared by giving ourselves fully creates a very different result. It depends on our intentions. If we serve out of a sense of obligation, or to get something back or to look good, we can expect a different outcome than when we serve with a pure heart. When we serve out of duty or obligation, we are doing something that we don't really want to do. If our heart is not behind the action, there won't be much energy. It will feel like work, not service. Often there will be an underlying resentment associated with the action. Things will get done, but because they were given with a forced energy they will not be received as a gift.

We don't have to look far to find people who could benefit from what we have to offer. It's just as easy to cook one chicken for ourselves as it is to put another chicken in the oven for the next-door neighbors who have just lost a beloved family member. This is not a duty, it is the extension of a kind and loving heart feeling compassion for what it is to be a human being. Offering the gift of service not only opens our hearts, but in the serving we open the hearts of others.

Even the most enlightened women are occasionally guilty of serving others but forgetting to serve themselves first. By honoring ourselves and our Spirit within, we actually have a great deal more energy to share our gifts with the world. We can only help others to the extent that we have looked after ourselves. When we are not connected to our Higher Selves, we can only offer what we have. Some days that is not much.

We know that the most meaningful activity in which we can be engaged is directly related to human evolution. But it is not enough now to be concerned only with our own evolution. Our attention must shift to the survival and evolution of all living things. We need to look after ourselves, and then we can truly be in service to others. What the world truly needs now is the service of hearts that have taken the time to connect with their deepest truths.

Musings & Blessings

HOW CAN WE BE IN SERVICE without putting more things to do on our plates? The most important thing is to teach by example. When you give of yourself, do so with a pure heart. Do small things for the love of another. Show simple kindnesses. An honest compliment, a sincere smile or a loving touch can go a long way in serving another by demonstrating compassion in action.

Sometimes when we look around at what is happening on the planet it can seem overwhelming. Where can we help? What can we give? Who do we have to be to make a difference? There is so much work to be done that it is difficult to know where to start.

To satisfy your soul's craving to serve, find something you love, something you feel passionate about. That way, when you encounter obstacles you will be able to dig deeper into the love that you are. You need not worry about being burnt out or getting tired if you are serving from a deep place of love and passion. Start close to home, and then expand your wings to include others as far away as you can, with joy in your heart.

A good place to start is to share your knowledge and wisdom with young women. Remind them of how powerful they are. Show them how they can make a difference in a world that so desperately needs their loving Feminine Hearts. That service is a great gift to the future of the world.

Breathe in your heart's desire. Exhale, offering your love to the world. Breathe in love.

If you think you are too small to have an impact, try going to bed with a mosquito.
– ANITA RODDICK –

The Gift of Sexuality

My Darling Feminine Heart:

Tonight he came to take me
to places not yet known.
He took my hand and held my heart
and together we soared to the next threshold …
that place of holy union
where together we became one.
Thank you, Goddess, for allowing me to surrender
my heart, body and soul to love's bliss.

> *Sexual love, energized by absolute love, is ecstasy.*
> — DEEPAK CHOPRA —

A S ENLIGHTENED WOMEN WE'VE HAD SEX, and then we've had *sex*. There were
times when we trusted our partner so deeply that the doors to our hearts
flew open, allowing the breath of other worlds to enter. There were also times
when the sexual experience was without a deeper heart-and-soul connection to
our intimate partners. We shared our bodies, but the experience was little more
than the exchange of bodily fluids.

Throughout my life, I have spoken with thousands of women about the
kinds of relationships they envisioned for themselves. Discussing their dreams
and their values was always a vital part of the conversation.

Every woman has her own idea of what is important, depending on her stage
of life and her experience in romantic in relationships. Women of a certain age
have distinct views about what they look for in relationships where they share
themselves sexually. Most aren't willing to settle for just sex. They have the

vibrators and other sex toys to satisfy their mere physical cravings. What they long for is a sexual relationship involving a gamut of experiences — including the emotional, physical and spiritual.

We have chosen to be here in the physical form as an expression of the Goddess, so we may as well have the deepest, most exquisite experience possible in our physical bodies. Our feminine essence is the same as the creative life force that is present in everything. This force (or spiritual energy) is intimately connected with our sexual energy, which is in turn connected with our Feminine Hearts. Consequently, if you want to have a sexual experience beyond the mundane — one that borders on the divine — it is imperative to share yourself with a deserving partner who you can trust.

Almost every woman I have ever talked to has said she would prefer sex with a heart connection than sex without it. (That doesn't include the dozens of sex workers I interviewed while in university writing a psychology paper on sexuality.) Some women don't understand that the sexual experience is quite different for the average man. Sure, a heart connection is nice, but it's not essential for him to have a very satisfying sexual experience.

If your partner has a strong sense of his masculine purpose, and you are very lucky, he can take you deeper into yourself. He can serve you by taking you closer to God than you can take yourself — or not. Ask yourself, "Does this man fill my heart so deeply that I am willing to share my body, my mind and my Spirit with him?"

You must choose. You always get to choose the person to whom you give your love. When you decide, give with total abandon and unconditional love. Remember, when you open your heart to love, the sexual sharing can awaken the experience of infinite love in both partners. When you are with your partner, offer a silent prayer that will bless both of you.

A Prayer for Him

My Darling:

When you take me,
do not leave any pieces behind.
All of me hungers to be connected to love's source;
not just pieces of me.
And when you take me
take me in the Spirit of love
honoring my soul as though it was your own.
When you take me ...
take me home.
Thank you, darling, for bringing me home
to that place where
I am one with God.

As accomplished women we have worked hard to achieve our levels of success
— but often, to realize our goals we've had to express our masculine essence. If
our sexual essence is mainly feminine, it is difficult to drop our masculine energy
at the door and switch into our Feminine Hearts as we walk through the entrance
to our homes.

Unfortunately, many women can't shift gears when they finally have some
quiet time to be intimate with their partners. After running the show all day,
they have difficulty giving up control and allowing their partner to lead. This
can wreak havoc in sexual relationships.

The Feminine Heart wants to give up making all the decisions. Many women
would love to let their partners take over, especially when it comes to intimate
exchanges. A woman wants to be with a man she can trust, so that she can
surrender to his masculine direction. The Feminine Heart needs a man who
will honor and treasure her soul, allowing her to attain life's greatest blessing
— the full experience of giving and receiving love. This is where the whirling
cosmos of the universe does its little tap dance. This is the moment when the

magic of life occurs. This is where your light can bless the man who basks in your radiance, in the process healing yourself.

"Whoever separated God from sex should be brought up for trial, charged with emotional crimes against humanity," trumpets Marianne Williamson, and I wholeheartedly agree. Some people have become blasé toward the myriad sexual messages thrown their way. The media, whether it hits us in the form of music, television or advertising, uses sex to sell products, and sell it does.

Working with teenagers was a real eye-opener for me. A male friend and I created a workshop for kids aged 14 to 17 to celebrate their sexual differences, and to honor each other for those differences. I spent most of the weekend working with the girls, while my friend worked with the boys. Throughout each day we would come together to celebrate and practice what we had learned.

Speaking to girls about their sexuality was unsettling for me. Many of these girls had had various forms of sexual contact with the opposite sex, but with very little thought about it.

"If he doesn't get sex from me, someone else will give it to him," one demure-looking girl shared with the group. "All the girls are giving oral sex," explained another sophisticated-looking 15-year-old. "What's the big deal?"

The big deal is this: if you are giving away one of the most sacred things that a man and woman can share together, it lessens the meaning of the sexual experience for everyone. Everybody loses when we view sex as a recreational activity, rather than as the holy experience that is available to us when we allow Spirit to enter the relationship.

The intimate sharing of masculine and feminine energy is a powerful force on every level. When we view our sexual relations as casual, we aren't making love with our hearts, only with our genitals. But there is nothing casual about opening ourselves up to the healing powers of the energetic polarities of the universe. We are playing with fire.

You cannot have another person enter your body, in any form, without taking on that person's energy — physically, emotionally and spiritually. Hormones released into our bodies when we have sex with a man create a chemical bond, whether we want that bond or not. Don't assume that your partner will experience the same physical and emotional bond that you do. This creates myriad misunderstandings between men and women regarding sexual relationships. Our intentions and experiences are often vastly different.

Sensitive, intuitive types (which many enlightened women are) take on a lot more than the "big kahuna" when they enter into a sexual relationship with a man. When you allow a man into your body, unless he has already entered your heart, the experience will be cold and lifeless.

When you allow a man into your body, unless he has already entered your heart, the experience will be cold and lifeless.

Expressing love sexually is actually one of the highest spiritual experiences we can share with another person. Opening ourselves wide to this life force takes us through all our darkest, most vulnerable places into the full expression of our hearts' emotions. This is not a place to play. We must be prepared to deal with all the old emotional patterns that will surface during the sexual sharing.

If you really want to have your batteries charged (which you probably do) attract a deserving man into your life and give him all the good loving that you can. Heal him with your love and radiance. Make him a better man because you believe in him. Tell him. Look into his eyes. With your right hand over his heart, tell him why you are blessed by his masculine presence. In turn, his maleness will seep into your skin, bathing you in the polarity of life: the whole experience.

This man, now blessed by your loving Spirit and open heart, has increased energy and fortitude to go out into the world and fight for his cause. Because he is a deserving man, his purpose will be worthwhile. His capacity to share what he has to contribute to the world will be further enhanced by the generous grace of your gift of sexuality.

When we open our hearts and Spirits to our sexual partner, magic happens. We can travel to places unknown that would be impossible to access on our own.

Musings & Blessings

HOW SATISFIED ARE YOU WITH THE QUALITY OF YOUR SEXUAL EXPRESSION? Does it meet the needs of your heart and soul as well as your physical desires? Honestly assess your intentions in entering into a sexual relationship with your partner. Is it to produce offspring, to satisfy hormonal cravings or to enter into the realm of spiritual bliss?

What is important is that you are aware of your intentions. When they are in alignment with your Feminine Heart, the sexual relationship can be a healing experience for everyone involved.

If in the process of your sexual loving you are not healing one another, you are hurting one another. There is already enough pain on the planet. Do not add to its demise, but surrender your heart to the possibility of a sexual union that will make the cosmos swoon.

Breathe in love, honor and respect for your partner and yourself. Exhale, breathing that feeling out into the world. Breathe in love.

... and here she was, her arms warm around him,
her mind snuggled beside his,
her scent wild and enticing and familiar.
The last guardian of his heart put down its shield ...
— NINA KIRIKI HOFFMAN —

The Gift of Surrender

My Darling Feminine Heart:

Just the thought of surrender
makes me quiver with fear.
What if I open my heart wide
and it is trampled on or abused?
What if I give my all
and it is not appreciated,
or worse, rejected?
When I go inside
and feel my love
I realize that I have nothing to fear.
For without my love
there is no surrendering.
I am safe.
I can choose to be safe
or I can choose to be fully alive
in the possibility that when
I surrender my heart
my fear disappears.
I am grateful, dear Goddess,
for I choose to surrender my love.

When opportunity for self-surrender arises, seizw it.
You will discover the secret in what you had hitherto tried to avoid;
indeed you will find even more.
— Thomas a Kempis —

REMEMBER HOW YOUR MOTHER USED TO SAY that you can tell a lot about a man by the way he leads you around the dance floor? Well, you can tell a lot about a woman by the way she follows him. I'm still learning how to follow a man around the dance floor, and it's finally coming with a semblance of grace as I learn to surrender to his purposeful direction.

One day I went for a run along a path cutting through the parkland forest as it followed the edge of a cool, clean lake. Huge tears rolled down my face as I connected with the divine force of God's love. I felt so grateful to be alive. Like crystal pearls of love, I felt the droplets on my cheeks. It was as though love's wetness was rolling down my cheeks. I felt surrendered to all of life, and it was heavenly.

During the rapture of sweet surrender in orgasm, the Feminine Heart is so opened up by the force of ecstatic love that tears will follow. It is difficult for some men to understand the depth of emotion in the Feminine Heart. If he loves, honors and respects you, however, he will allow his own heart to be opened by your love. Through sharing your love, he will be healed. The depth of that kind of surrender is the Feminine Heart's way of letting her Creator enter her mind, body and spirit.

One of the biggest lessons women must learn is how to surrender to their highest truth. To have faith that our inner voice of knowing is providing messages that serve takes courage. It becomes easier with practice, however.

When I mention the word surrender to women, I can see the fear creeping into their eyes. It is as though I've suggested that they give up their lives and everything that they've worked so hard to acquire and maintain. Women with overused and overdeveloped masculine sides have the most difficulty surrendering to their Feminine Hearts. We are so concerned with protecting ourselves. Afraid to let our hearts become vulnerable, we coat them with layers of fear. Like an onion's skin, we add layer upon layer of fear that we feel will somehow protect us from others, and from ourselves. All the reasons why we should shut down our hearts show up — fear of betrayal, fear of rejection, fear of abandonment, fear of not being good enough, fear of being too powerful — you name it. We feel that fear is necessary to protect our tender hearts.

Without surrender there can be no movement, no opening of the heart, no letting love in or out — the thing that the Feminine Heart most desires. We may have to reframe what it means to surrender to another; not seeing it as giving something up, but rather as letting something in.

One of my spiritual teachers has spent much of his life traveling around the world working mostly with woman who are experiencing a deep sense of emptiness and despair. Gurugi feels that the despair of Western women is because their big egos do not allow them to surrender to love's calling. "The problem for most Western women," he says matter-of-factly, "is that they don't know how to surrender themselves to God, to their men, or to anything."

"He doesn't know how hard Western women have worked to gain their independence and equality," I thought to myself. All the freedoms and opportunities that we have today came from protecting ourselves, from taking care of ourselves and fighting for the right to have the same kick at the can that men have.

In some workshops I've taught, surrender is one of the things we work on. It is not an idea that comes easily to most women, especially the most accomplished, self-sufficient and independent women. It's paradoxical. We crave closeness, connection and intimacy with our partners, friends and Spirit, yet we are unwilling to surrender our hearts to the experience. If we can get over the idea that we won't lose anything in the process of surrendering our hearts to another, then we can begin to see the rewards that are available — not only for us, but for the people whose lives we touch.

Surrender is the path to having heartfelt experiences. It is also one of the greatest gifts we have to offer our men, our families and our friends.

AN ATTRACTIVE 40-SOMETHING WOMAN named Jennifer attended one of my workshops on surrendering. She held a responsible, high-profile position as a CEO for a major corporation. Many people relied on her, and she felt personally responsible to the shareholders in her company. The first night of the workshop she was convinced that if she surrendered her heart, she would somehow become weakened. "I have to be on purpose and strong-minded at all times," she lamented earnestly. "How does surrender work for a woman in my position?"

Remember, we are not our jobs, or our positions. The more responsibility and authority we have in our careers, the more we seem to forget this…until we get home from work. Then we let down our hair, pull off our pantyhose and just want to *be* ourselves. Unfortunately, we have become so accustomed to fighting the impulse to surrender that even when we get home we can't surrender to the flow of life. We continue trying to control everything and everyone who crosses our paths.

Position has nothing to do with our ability to be open-hearted in our daily affairs. We can still manage our responsibilities while keeping our hearts open to the beating pulse of the universe. We can still breathe in the life force and engage with the truth that we know ourselves to be, while making decisions and meeting deadlines. We must remain aware of our intentions. Do our decisions come from within? Are they for the highest good of everyone involved? When we come from that place, decisions become easier. Surrendering to our own inner wisdom in business requires that we trust ourselves and trust the process. Surrendering is not something that we *do*, but it has everything to do with who we are *being*.

Many martial arts experts use the energy of their opponents to deflect any harm coming toward them by surrendering to the flow of their opponents' energy. Become a feminine warrior and surrender to the flow of life's energy as you battle through the day's activities. You will remain centered and much less fatigued at the day's end than if you fight against the flow of life.

If you truly respect that divine aspect that you are, you will not tolerate the crushing of your Spirit at the hands of a man to whom you have surrendered your heart. You do not have to get angry — just don't give the man any more of your time. Unless of course, he acknowledges his brutishness and promises on a stack of flowers that he will not treat you that way again. And he doesn't.

After you have made a commitment for life with someone and that person has hurt you several times, the pain starts to become unbearable. Like thick layers of an onion, you start to wrap layers around your gentle heart. It helps dull the pain. Sometimes the temptation is to use alcohol, drugs, food or shopping — anything to dull the pain (a nice, rich ice cream seems to be a big hit!). We all have our own favorite "drug" that we use to medicate ourselves.

There are other choices, of course. I hope you will choose another option — like breathing. Breathe in deeply and exhale, letting go of your anger, betrayal, sadness, or whatever troubles your soul — opening up your body while feeling in your deepest heart. Share the truth of what you are feeling. Not your story about it, just how it made you feel. Own your truth. Ask for what you need or don't need, and be clear about it. The masculine can, in his clear consciousness, respond to your request or not.

Only you can choose when it is time to take action, and what action to take. Just be clear that you are a daughter of the Goddess and remember why you are here — to give and receive love. If you're not getting it, get out or change the situation. Both are daunting tasks requiring great courage. But we're not talking about taking out the garbage here, we're talking about your heart. There is enough pain and suffering in the world without contributing to our planet's emotional suffering. If there are children around, I request that you be extra vigilant. They do not need to see the worst of what the sexes can do to each other. They need to see the possibility of deep love and respect between men and women so that they can choose wisely when their time comes to select a loving partner.

You cannot surrender without breathing properly. You've got to breathe deeply, releasing whatever doesn't look like love as you exhale. There are different levels of surrender, but you can really move things quickly if you start at the densest level, the physical level. Let go. Get a massage and shake out the tension — do anything that allows you to release your physical tension — and your emotional and spiritual body will be opened more quickly. Remember to breathe. Breathe in your blessings. Breathe in love and life, and savor the flavor.

Musings & Blessings

ARE YOU WORKING FROM YOUR HEAD OR YOUR HEART? What's the worst thing that could happen if you opened up your heart and tenderly offered it to someone, or something? The object of your trust might betray you. Perhaps you might fail at a certain project. Yes, it stings. The immediate, learned response is to once again shut down your heart, adding another protective layer just for good measure. Heart opening is an exercise. Like any new skill it takes practice, time and perseverance. Breathe in deeply from your feminine core. Breathe in and trust yourself enough to let go … .

Trust and its sister, surrender, are like a womb
in which all of consciousness can gestate and mature.
– RICHARD MOSS –

The Gift of Touch

My Darling Feminine Heart:

When I share a gentle touch
my body reacts
my heart sighs
my soul sings.
The greatest gift of physical touch
is that it deeply touches the heart too.
Thank you, Goddess, for the healing power of touch.

Nothing can cure the soul but the senses,
just as nothing can cure the senses but the soul.
— Oscar Wilde —

ONE OF THE EASIEST AND SIMPLEST GIFTS the Feminine Heart can offer is the gift of touch. Touch is one of the most delicate of all the human senses. After smell, it is one of the first sensory systems to develop in infancy. Research has proven that touch is linked to physical and mental development, creating a strong self-identity and healthy interpersonal relationships. Regardless of someone's age, touch can communicate comfort, affection and support — something we all need daily.

The technological explosion invading our homes and lives leaves us more alienated from others than ever before in history. Consequently, we are more touch-deprived than at any time in history. The more technologically advanced the society, the more touch-deprived its people.

Years ago, while still in university, I wrote a paper for a psychology course entitled, "The Need For Touch." My theory was that the occurrence of sexually transmitted diseases would be greatly reduced if people had more opportunities to freely touch one another. Many women can recall a time when we agreed to a sexual encounter beyond what our hearts told us was appropriate because we so yearned for intimacy and connection. Sexually transmitted diseases are on the rise, and research shows that the incidence is highest among young women who have had several sexual partners. For those of us past a certain age, when the blush is no longer on the rose, it may be difficult to feel compassion. In our wisdom, however, we know what these women are looking for — to be touched and to connect with another (and consequently themselves) on a deeper level.

Touch is vital for a healthy life. Our kids crave it. Our animals need it. Many adults anesthetize themselves with addictions so they don't feel the need to connect with other human beings so acutely. Many of our elderly are dying faster than they need to, simply because of a lack of touch.

When we touch another human being, we are connecting at a deep, primal level. When our dear cat Oreo was still alive, he made sure that he got his touch fix by wiping his sleek body up against us whenever he got a chance. Some days when I was particularly preoccupied poor Oreo got fed, but not much else. No problem. He demanded that we met his need for touch. My son and I would watch in amazement as he pried our hands away from us with his paws whenever he wanted a good petting.

Anthropological studies show that cultures who demonstrate less affection, also tend to be more violent than cultures where physical touching is deemed more acceptable. In our technologically sophisticated societies, the simple act of touch could positively affect our daily lives. Violence has become commonplace. Intimacy could be commonplace as well, if we spent more time focusing on spreading the healing balm of our feminine touch.

Before the AIDS era, people had sex to alleviate the deep yearning for intimate connection with others. Women especially seemed to need intimacy, and would satisfy their cravings by consenting to have sex. Of course, they always had to face the emotional ramifications of giving themselves to men who did not respect their need to be held, cuddled and touched, but who were more concerned about relieving their sexual urges. It was the price these women paid.

The Feminine Heart knows when she gives herself to a less-than-deserving man — a man whose purpose and mission in life does not serve the woman she knows herself to be. You must be clear about who you are, so that you attract a man you know deserves your care and attention.

Working as a massage therapist for years, I was aware of the healing that took place through the intimacy of being touched. I put myself through university while working in my massage practice. Studying psychology while working as a therapist, I had numerous opportunities to reflect on the impact of massage on the minds, bodies and spirits of my clients.

It was obvious that one of the greatest side benefits of the massage was the experience my clients had of opening up to another human and receiving from that person. While I was administering the massage, people would often share how much they needed to be touched, and that the experience was "better than sex." I realized that sexually transmitted diseases would be far less prevalent if people were touched regularly. This was the early 1980s, however, when AIDS wasn't the threat that it is today.

Although it is slowly changing, women have a lot more freedom than men do to touch each other. The Feminine Heart knows how healing her touch can be, and will share her gift freely with others. Holding the hand of a scared child, rubbing the back of a tired friend, or stroking the head of a sick parent can alleviate a world of ills.

The messages out there are confusing. The media has kids neurotic about their sexuality, mainly because we don't have many really positive role models who are strong in their sexual essence. As well, growing bodies of research suggest that North American children and adolescents are dangerously touch-deprived. School counselors and psychologists report that today's pervasive sexual-abuse allegations are major barriers to how we view touch.

"It's a very serious problem. If monkeys are deprived of touch, they kill each other," reported Tiffany Field, director of the University of Miami's Touch Research Institute, in a recent publication. "I think parents really need to make sure kids are getting some touch, a back rub before they go to bed or while they're doing their homework."

Innately we know that our infants and children need touch, and we do it instinctively. When a baby cries, we pick it up and pat its back. When a child falls and comes screaming to us with a scraped knee, we "kiss it better." Over the years I was curious about children who grow up in touch-deprived environments, such as orphanages, where little human contact is the norm. Not surprisingly, the results are devastating. The souls of these little creatures are severely dispirited.

Verbally or through body language, our children let us know how much touching, and what kind of touching, they require. Teens want and need touch and affection — yet they often pull away from our offerings. As they explore their own sexual essence, they develop boundaries that include their parents' touch. When we respect their wishes they feel empowered, but don't stop offering your healing hands. Just knowing that you are there is the most important thing for them at this stage of their lives.

Working with teenagers in a workshop setting dealing with masculine and feminine sexual essence gave me much insight into the need for touch, for belonging, for being accepted. Young women shared their fears and their intense loneliness. Why they shared their tender young bodies with men and boys who never acknowledged a glimmer of their radiant Spirits was no mystery to me. When these girls were feeling sad or bad about themselves, they were not interested in a sexual relationship. What they craved was the feeling of intimacy, closeness and love. Sex was a substitute for what their Feminine Hearts really desired.

Young women greatly need to understand their Feminine Hearts. They can be taught how to love and respect themselves so that they get their needs met while retaining their honor. Take the time to share your knowledge and wisdom with the young people in your life. Make sure to give them a hug or a cuddle while you are at it, and watch them flourish.

A S WE ENTER ADULTHOOD, we seem to reserve touch for those who we are intimately connected with. Touch is a big part of an intimate relationship, but it need not be reserved for the object of our romantic affections. As a group, the elderly are in the most touch-deprived sector of our society. With their families living across the country, many elderly people receive only the most rudimentary touching, if any. Perhaps that is why so many studies are done on the benefits of animals in nursing homes, measuring the benefits when the inhabitants are able to touch a living entity that can respond. As enlightened women, we know this intuitively. That is why we reach out to others not only with our love, but with our hands. We have the power to heal with our loving touch.

My maternal grandfather suffered a serious stroke and lived the last two years of his life in the hospital. Receiving only rudimentary care from overworked and restricted hospital personnel, he didn't receive any touching. Even my dedicated mother, who daily brought him home-cooked meals, did not feel free in her relationship to touch him more than through the process of caring for his rudimentary feeding and clothing needs. Expressing love physically was not a cultural norm for either of them; they showed their love in other ways. Food was a safe way to express love, appreciation and caring.

I always made a point of visiting my grandfather in the hospital when I went to the city. Living a day's drive from my family, I was only able to visit twice or three times a year. He would light up when he saw me enter his room, and my heart would melt when I saw the fragments of the strong man that I knew sitting feebly in his bed, where he spent almost every hour of every day.

Stroking his almost-bald head while talking to him would send tears rolling down his grizzled cheeks. I would massage his shoulders and back, his hands and arms, knowing he was receiving so much more than the circulatory benefits that massage provides. While his stagnated body relished in the health benefits of my massage techniques, his broken spirit soared from the love I was able to communicate through touch.

M Y MOTHER TOLD ME THAT SHE BELIEVED the reason he lived for so long after his stroke is that he would wait patiently for the next time I would come to visit. The intimacy we shared while I was touching him kept him grounded enough in his body to remain on the planet.

The elderly are getting ready to leave the physical world and move on to the Spiritual realm. With your loving intention, whether through an intimate gaze, a genuine smile or a loving touch, you can make their last days on the planet meaningful. It is one of the gifts that you have to offer. Give freely, and the rewards will come back to you in spades.

As people have evolved, they realize that they need touch and don't have to wait for a sexual encounter to have the deep experience that touching others offers. Some people have created gatherings that facilitate the need to be touched or to be held. Many people attend workshops or gatherings where they go into a room full of strangers and semi-strangers and by the end of it leave having had intimate connections with others. Whether through touch, holding or gazing deeply into one another's eyes, participants leave feeling connected to others who were recent strangers — they also leave feeling more connected to themselves and to all of humanity.

A trend originating out of New York to satisfy this need for touch is called the cuddle party.

The intention of these get-togethers across North America is to satisfy our craving for the intimacy of sex without actually having sex.

"A cuddle party is an event for adults to come together to practice welcomed touch and affectionate play and not have it be sexualized," reported Reid Mihalko, a Manhattan massage therapist and sex educator, in a recent news article.

These "cuddle puddles" or "cuddle fests" of intertwined bodies have been going on in various forms for years, at slumber parties, raves and retreats. The intention is similar to the love-ins of the 1960s, sans the sex. The week-long communal Burning Man festival at Black Rock Desert in Nevada has specific domes and pools set up to facilitate group cuddling. A good friend returned from the love fest amazed at the pervasive feeling of love and connectedness between strangers. But it isn't necessary to attend one of these events to bring more touch into your life and the lives of others — just extend your hand and somebody will take it.

Hugs are a wonderful way to touch someone. Try different types and lengths of hugs. Notice which hug you like best and when, if ever, you want to stop. Don't worry about your hug being accepted by other people — when their comfort level has been satiated, they will step back.

Try cupping someone's face gently between your hands, looking gently into his or her eyes and sending love. This is a very tender gesture that can assist the lucky recipient to actually experience a change of state.

When you are with a special man, place your right hand over his heart while talking or listening to him. You will be communicating at a much deeper level, and bringing him back into his body. This gift that you can give the masculine benefits everyone.

The next time you run into someone you care about, make an effort to connect through touch in the first few moments of getting together. This will immediately open up the quality of connection, making it possible to reach each other on a deeper level.

Musings & Blessings

How often each day do you extend your hand to someone? A gentle touch, a little rub or a heartfelt hug can make a huge difference in someone's life. People and animals automatically move away if you are unwelcome in their space. Trust your intuition, knowing you will offer what is needed. Whether the recipient is willing to receive your tender expression of love, he or she is always in need of it.

Breathe in gentle thoughts of kindness and love. Exhale. Breathe in love.

When you touch someone with loving hands, you touch their heart as well.
— JENICA ASHLIE —

The Gift of Wisdom

My Darling Feminine Heart:

There is so much that I can share.
Within me, I carry the knowledge
and wisdom of the ages.
When I trust myself I don't need to prove
myself to anyone.
My wisdom comes from a place
beyond books and degrees.
The wisdom I possess
was shared by angels and saints.
This is the wisdom
that was given to me at birth.
It is in love and gratitude
that I give thanks to Goddess for the gift of wisdom.

Women ... are born three thousand years old.
— SHELAGH DELANEY —

THROUGHOUT OUR LIVES WE LEARN AND GROW, but the main focus of any work a woman takes on is the discovery of her true self, and the balance between her masculinity and femininity. We may achieve this on our own or, more likely, through our relationships. It may be through the exploration of our sexuality, which takes us into unexpected depths and requires us to reach an understanding of our own spirituality. It may appear in our dreams.

As we journey through the various stages of life, we are presented with different gifts of learning and challenges, each gift bringing us closer to our true selves. We bring the wisdom of the ages with us throughout life's phases. During the different stages our focus and understanding is different. Each gift comes in its own time. They are all life's blessings.

In our maiden years as tumultuous teenagers, we learn how to handle the first phase of womanhood. We dream of all the things that we will do, or be. Experimenting with all our new-found knowledge and awareness gives life an exciting quality that can lead to the exploration of things that really matter. As well as coming to terms with bodily changes and an emerging sexuality, every maid needs to develop her relationship with her own spirituality — that deep connection between oneself as a physical being and the ultimate wisdom and infinite intelligence that is available to everyone.

When a young woman takes the time to feel her energy within, she begins to develop her intuition. As her awareness expands, she becomes more adept and able to speak her truths with conviction. During this time a maid finds her sleep overtaken by dreams, helping her handle the energies within. Her quest is to find balance, as she comes to terms with herself as a newly awakened sexual and spiritual being.

From a sexual perspective, she is learning to understand her own need for companionship and closeness with the others around her. Many of her dreams will echo the intense feelings she has about people and situations, dreams that demonstrate how to work with those feelings. Often she will be overwhelmed by the vast energy and power available to young women at this stage. It may be a tumultuous time, for her and for those around her. She is learning how to reconcile her sexual and spiritual polarities, and in the process, how to become complete and whole.

OUR SOCIETY BLURS THE DISTINCTIONS between the different phases of a woman's life, but the phase of maid traditionally ends with a woman's first pregnancy. This is the transition into motherhood.

The mother stage is an active and creative time in a woman's life, although this may have nothing to do with having babies.

Today the need to marry and procreate is not so pressing. However, the choice of freedom is not to be exchanged lightly for the responsibilities of a family. The days are gone when the roles of men and women, and the division of labor, were clear-cut. Women who have chosen career and motherhood still bear the larger share of child care responsibility, and must find a balance between home, office and the children.

Many women today choose not to have children, or to delay the process until they are older, so they fill their mothering role in other ways. These women may choose to find fulfillment through their careers, or through voluntary work. Whatever path we choose in our lives, during the mother phase of our lives we need to become more aware of our principles and beliefs, so we can pass these values on to the new lives that we have created.

In our wisdom, we must find the balance between our sexuality and our preoccupation with our children. During this time our focus tends to move away from ourselves and centers on our children—how and what they will be, or how we will participate in that unfolding.

Our dreams (which often serve the purpose of trying to instruct or compensate) may present us with those parts of our personality that we are trying to come to terms with. We may dream of our own mothers as we try to balance the positive and negative aspects of all the feminine archetypes that we have encountered throughout our lives. Often it is in our dreams, when symbols of fertility emerge into figures of wisdom, that we get the first sign that we are transitioning into the next phase of life — the mature, wise woman.

MANY TERMS ARE USED TO DESCRIBE THE LAST PHASE of a woman's life, none of which I find useful. The terms crone and hag (which means blessed) often portray an old, wizened, arthritic figure. A woman was considered a crone when she needed to attend to her own concerns, as her children had grown and her husband had passed on. For her, this was a time to develop new wisdom derived from her experience and knowledge.

As a single mother for more than 10 years, I see how I have lived my 40s like a crone. Many women are on their own today. Either by choice or by circumstance, they have been doing everything on their own for some time. However, this is not natural for the feminine expression. That is why many older women choose to live together, or to live in closer proximity to other women. We need to feel supported in our lives so that we can give more of our greatest gifts.

When we are on our own our feminine energy is not fully expressed — we feel and look older than we should. As we lose our radiance our features become more angular; our feminine softness disappears and we start to lose our vitality.

At this stage, the wise woman is no longer concerned with procreation so she can channel her creative energy in other ways. If she finds that her sexual interest has waned, she can concentrate on her (and her partner's) needs for love and affection, and find different ways to express her sexuality and sensuality. If her libido increases, she can find creative ways to channel that energy.

Each woman will find her own way of handling the different energies that become apparent at this stage of life. Aspects of her personality may arise that she didn't have the time to notice or experience before. She may express these newly felt urges with the grace of wisdom or, as she experiments with different ways of being, the outrageousness of an adolescent.

Establishing balance in her life is the most important thing a mature woman can do for herself, and for those around her. Most of the Goddesses associated with maturity have strong dual natures — and every mortal woman has experienced this as well. Her gentle, loving matriarchal ways, where she is able to clearly perceive the needs of others within her family or group, are met by a darker, destructive side. It is not until we fully embrace and understand the true power of the darker side that we can attain the wisdom and perception of the truly wise.

The enlightened woman walks a tightrope. Either she lives in her full power radiating God's light, or she is pulled into the struggle of bitterness and destruction. With every expression of the feminine, the woman of years must come to terms with the destructive side of her being and, if she has not already done so, transform that energy. Fears, doubts, guilt, past traumas — the full spectrum must be embraced with an open heart and forgiven. Otherwise, these demons will continue to be expressed in our dreams and in our waking hours.

Out of this transformation arises the twin gifts of wisdom and clarity of perception. During this stage we find ourselves dreaming about things we have not been able to do before. We feel the need to express parts of our personality that we have kept dormant. A sense of urgency arises.

As our feminine sexual essence changes yet again, we realize awareness of the true union we have been searching for. The outward expression of our search for connection with others lessens. As we let go and surrender to the flow of life's pace, we have a much larger perspective. We have faced life bravely, and our hearts have opened and closed many, many times. We have learned that we are at our best, and our highest, when our hearts remain open to ourselves and to others.

Our purpose changes as well. With our new clarity of perception, we see what needs to be done in service to humanity. No longer as concerned with our immediate dependants, we can help others understand and take responsibility for their actions. We don't need to have everything anymore. We are more concerned with *being* our greatest gift.

Before we can truly help others, however, we must have developed the intention of service, as is God's will. That is a career that can last a lifetime.

As we move though life's stages, our work and responsibilities change. At each stage, we have access to that eternal wisdom that is ours. Find ways to express the wisdom that you possess. Regardless of your age, or your stage in life, you can experience those aspects of your journey if it is in your destiny.

Musings & Blessings

WHEN DO YOU FIND YOURSELF DOUBTING YOURSELF? When have you known something to be true but held your tongue, not wanting to share your wisdom out of fear of being judged or criticized?

With a pure heart, wisdom is available to the Feminine Heart at all stages of life. Embrace the stage of life that you are now experiencing. It is all perfect. Breathe in deeply and give thanks for being here, now, at this time in the planet's evolution. Give thanks for the wisdom that you have to offer as we enter into a new era of love. Breathe in love.

Believe nothing because it is written in books,
Believe nothing because wise men say it is so.
Believe nothing because it is a religious doctrine.
Believe only because you yourself know it to be true.
– BUDDHA –

Part Three

Deep Passion

Offering the Gift of Endless Love

A Legacy of Love

My Darling Feminine Heart:

Please allow the beauty and radiance
that fills my heart to
bless the lives of all who witness
the brilliance of my love's healing light.
This light is the gift of love that I offer
to change the lives of all
who bask in its luminescent glow.
Use me as a beacon to others
when they have lost their way in the dark
or strayed off the path to their Highest Selves.
Give me the wisdom, courage and strength
to share my light and offer the shelter of my wings
even when I am tired, discouraged and empty.
Show me the way to keep my light burning brightly
so that my love is reflected into the eyes of others.
Thank you, Goddess, for your blessing of a passionate life.

Life without passion is nothing more than a broken promise.
— BARBARA RASKIN —

THE FEMININE HEART HUNGERS TO FEEL THAT HER LIFE MATTERS. She craves the comfort of knowing that her personal mark on Mother Earth will remain long after she has gone. We all offer our own unique set of gifts, and we want to leave the imprint of those gifts behind for others. How we do that is a personal choice. What is important is that we do something to make a difference. In the end, we want to know that our lives mattered.

When we don't live as though we have a purpose, life begins to look meaningless. We stop and wonder, "What am I doing this for?" The day-to-day grind becomes just that, a daily grinding that wears us down. Our radiance begins to dull, and before we know it we are the living dead. We go through the motions of living with little or no joy, satisfaction or passion.

In Part One we saw that having a connection to our Creator is key to finding fulfillment in our daily lives. The quality of this relationship is what colors our daily experiences. This is what sustains us and gives meaning to our endless pursuits and activities.

The intention of Part Two was to serve as a guide to many of the gifts that we have to offer others. In our offerings, we are actually reinforcing the truth of who we are. The more we give, the more we receive the knowing of what we are made of, the truth of our Higher Selves.

In Part Three you will discover how to keep that light burning brightly so that others may benefit.

Whether you are at home, at work or volunteering at your child's school, the quality of what you offer to the people around you is based on the love that you carry within your heart.

To leave a legacy, we must find ways of expressing the truth of our Highest Selves. Whether in the work we do, our volunteer efforts, or how we raise our children, the way we express our deepest Feminine Heart is what will be left behind.

If you are not already embracing your passion, it may take a little soul searching, or a dramatic life event, to expose your truth. The important thing is not how you come about finding your passion, but that you do. It is waiting there, like an untapped source of energy. Acknowledge it, and release it. It will become your legacy of love.

Our lives today are full. Many of us are pushed to the maximum, every day. Many of us give so much to our jobs and careers that the people we love receive only what we have left at the end of the day — and some days that is not much. Yet we know that life is short and precious, and we long to make a difference. We have the power and wisdom to make big changes. By contributing the best of what we have to offer, without compromise, we can make a difference in our families, our organizations and ultimately, by banding together, in the world.

The intention of Part Three is to help empower you to do the things for yourself that will have the biggest impact on others — today, tomorrow and in the days to come, long after your time on this planet has come to an end. The thought I want to emphasize is that you don't have to do everything on your own. Each time a Feminine Heart shares her light, it helps brighten the radiance of all people. At this time in our planet's history, with darkness prevalent, working together we can illuminate the world with a light it has never before seen. This light is the power of your radiant Feminine Heart to create a new era of love.

Our Light, Brightly Burning

My Darling Feminine Heart:

I wake up each day and go about my life
fulfilling my obligations, responsibilities and chores
to my family, my job and my friends.
Some days, I even look after myself.
When my heart is open and my love shines forth
I attract the people, situations and events
that help to make things flow more easily…
with less effort and struggle.
I see the gratitude on the faces
of the people who received my love
when it was offered with a radiant heart.
They are blessed by my offerings.
Thank you, Goddess, for the gentle reminder
that even the smallest gift can make the biggest difference
when given in the intention of my healing and nurturing love.

As far as we can discern, the sole purpose of human existence
is to kindle a light in the darkness of mere being.
— Carl Jung —

WE LONG TO BE CONNECTED TO SPIRIT. Only spiritual teachings that direct us inward can help heal our sense of separation. The planet is suffering from the effects of our lack of connection. We don't have to look far to see the effects of a world that has lost its belief in the goodness of humanity.

Strangers in public places are afraid to make eye contact with others. We are a fear-based society. The light workers of this planet can share their love, and light up the fear-filled paths that many people stumble along. It is a big job, but working together, each doing our part, it becomes easier — and the momentum is incredible.

Conscious awareness will be required to make new choices. But they are not difficult ones once we make the decision and set our intention as to how we will proceed.

As I mentioned earlier in this book, there were times that I stopped subscribing to the daily newspaper. Every morning for about a month, our local newspaper featured cover stories about the terror facing people in Serbia, Bosnia and other war-torn countries. Starting my day staring at a wide-eyed child who'd just witnessed a swath of evil descending on his family made my stomach roll. Looking at the grizzled face of a woman whose heart was ripped out of its socket watching soldiers torture her children was more than my psyche could tolerate as part of my breakfast menu.

In today's world, focusing on the negative seems to be what many people find entertaining. It takes a concerted effort to stay focused on the good that exists. To keep that light burning brightly, find places, people and situations that fill your heart's desire. Express your passion so that your health and happiness will be fully realized.

What things can you do to bring more light into your life? You may have to change some of your activities, or change some friendships. How can you consciously protect yourself from the negativity that is so pervasive in our culture? Are you willing to turn off the television when an inane sitcom comes blaring into your family room? Are you willing to forgive a transgression made by a friend, or the betrayal of an ex-lover? Are you willing to do what it takes to keep your light burning brightly? Only you can answer these questions.

Is it your destiny to co-create with Spirit to bring more light and love into the world? You will suffer, knowing that you are not living your highest calling if it is within your power. Every woman, no matter her station in life, has been given a gift that longs to be expressed. It may be something that does not seem that it will make a big difference in the scope of what needs to be done to make changes on our planet. But if you can make a difference in your own sphere of influence — in your home, your community or your place of work — what you are doing is no less important than the work of angels.

In her book *Conscious Evolution*, Barbara Marx Hubbard uses a quote from the *Gospel According to Thomas* that captures this thought: "If you bring forth what is within you, what you bring forth will save you. If you do not bring forth what is within you, what you do not bring forth will destroy you."

It's always about choice. Choose wisely.

Musings & Blessings

WHEN HAVE YOU FELT THAT YOU WERE LIVING the full expression of who you really are? Do you express your passion as fully as you can, or do you hold back, waiting for a more "appropriate" time? When you ration your passion, what are you saving it for?

The only time you can fully express your passion is when you are *being* in the moment. Living in the past, or the future, has no power or passion. That is why breathing is so important. With each breath that comes in and goes out, you can experience connection with your Spirit. This connection allows your full expression of passion to manifest. Breathing in love and sharing it with the world as you exhale creates magic.

Breathe in your creative life force. Circulate that energy throughout your body. Exhale and express your passion. Breathe in love.

If I can stop one heart from breaking,
I shall not live in vain;
If I can ease one life the aching,
Or cool one pain,
Or help one fainting robin
Unto his nest again,
I shall not live in vain.
— EMILY DICKINSON —

Finding Work that Serves

My Darling Feminine Heart:

When my working day is over
I sit back and wonder,
did I make a difference today,
or was I just going through the motions?
I know that I have a special purpose
to share with the world.
No one like me has come before
and there will never be another me to come.
My purpose and the way that I express
my gifts are unique, never to be replicated.
I see the possibilities
where I can share my vision
of a better world.
Please, Goddess, help me
express my greatest gifts
as an offering to the world.
Thank you for helping me
find and follow my bliss.

Your work is to discover your work and then with all your heart to give yourself to it.
— BUDDHA —

IN THE LATE 1980s I STARTED WORKING IN THE CORPORATE WORLD as a
management consultant for one of the large international accounting firms
in the areas of training and development, re-employment counseling, and strategic

quality management. This opened up a whole world of women to me, women who were not only working in a "man's world" but who were trying to have another life outside of work.

With a Western psychology background, I started putting statistics and numbers together. I compared my health and happiness to other women I met. As a consultant, I worked with people from a variety of companies and industries. I studied their lifestyles, their attitudes, their demographics and their levels of happiness. I saw a lot of fatigue. This feeling of fatigue did not necessarily come from working hard, but from putting in days where their hearts were not engaged. With decent paychecks and the security of benefits dangling in front of their noses, these people had taken on work for which they were not well-suited, in environments that were actually detrimental to their well-being.

In my workshop "Working With Passion," many participants became agitated when I told them that spending their days working just for money was almost the same as prostitution. My clients didn't like the sound of that. However, it was interesting to see what they brought back to our next counseling session. The clients who had pondered this concept carefully, in the context of what they wanted out of their careers, were willing to become possibility thinkers. They realized that whatever you value highly makes a difference in job and life satisfaction.

Finding a company or organization that reflects your personal values — rather than just taking the first job that comes along — may take a little more time, but the payoffs are huge. Yes, the remuneration we receive from the service we provide is important, but after the paycheck is spent — then what? The amount of time we spend getting dressed for work, commuting to and from work, doing the work and then thinking about work once we get home, has a huge impact on the rest of our daily lives. Over time the incessant drive to do more with less, to improve productivity and bottom-line numbers, deflates the Feminine Heart. When do we have time to honor our personal and spiritual values in the workplace?

I consider Ann Coombs, author of *The Living Workplace*, to be a light worker in the area of workplace issues. "My definition of a toxic workplace is one without human relationships," she says in her book.

As well, in a recent interview with CanWest News Service, she said, "I was seeing a total disregard for spiritual and personal values — truth, honesty, thoughtfulness, graciousness — in the workplace."

This does not make for a fulfilled life for the Feminine Heart. The majority of people are not happy in their current jobs. Earlier, in Part One, we saw that approximately 60 per cent of women who responded to Oprah's questionnaire about their levels of happiness rated themselves only 6 out of 10. I believe these numbers reveal the struggle many women are experiencing today. This struggle is the tension between the realities of their work lives and their life purpose.

Many women are struggling with what they most value and what they do at work. The deep desire of the Feminine Heart to give and receive love is often lost in our places of employment.

While many progressive companies are now searching for ways to help employees maintain balance in their lives, it is a slow process. Not everyone is fortunate enough to work for a company that recognizes employees' needs as a priority.

Ann Coombs lists four ways to recognize spirituality in the workplace:

1. Honor the Creator who exists in all human beings.
2. Respect and develop human potential.
3. Pursue and support excellence at every level.
4. Share profits.

Sounds simple and straightforward, but old habits die hard.

IN ALL MY YEARS AS A CAREER COUNSELOR, I never met anyone who didn't like a job if it involved something he or she loved doing. I have always felt that the luckiest people were those who would do a job even if there were no paycheck attached to it. When you love what you do you are probably good at it, and your enjoyment is obvious. People want to do business with you because you are a pleasure to work with, and what you produce is a gift of love.

To climb up the corporate ladder, women have had to make sacrifices to their radiant Feminine Hearts. We've learned to embrace our masculine sides. We've learned to take care of ourselves, rung after excruciating rung. We've learned to lead, but we're tired of doing it without a higher purpose. Day after day we show up at work feeling tired and used, our hearts suffering.

There was a saying pinned up in one of the offices where I used to work. "To get paid the same as man around here, you need to do your job twice as well — fortunately for me, that isn't difficult!"

Many women have toughed it out, competing with the old guard in the *Boys Club*, but at what cost? As Fawn Germer reminds us in her book *Hard Won Wisdom* (2001), that the median income of women is still just 73 cents on the dollar compared to men, even though the law has required equal pay since 1963.

A project by the Heinz Family Philanthropies and the Mellon Financial Corporation (2002) produced these facts:

- In 2000, the median income of women over age 65 was roughly half the income of men over 65.
- Two-thirds of the 7.2 million elderly women who live alone have incomes below $15,000.
- As a result of caregiving the average woman loses as much as $650,000 during her lifetime in missed promotions, raises and contributions to retirement plans.
- Social Security is the sole source of income for 25 per cent of older women.
- Only one in four divorced women collects pension benefits from her former spouse.

These statistics reflect the financial situations of women over a lifetime. What about the emotional and physical environments, both of which affect the Feminine Heart's feelings of satisfaction?

Many women in business tend to attack problems like men. Hardened by their actions, they become known as ball-busters. As an enlightened businesswoman, the only thing you should bust open is your heart, and the hearts of others. Help others in the workplace to come from their hearts. Share your deepest gifts while performing your daily responsibilities. The workplace is a great venue to practice heart-opening exercises because we spend so much of our time there. No matter what the culture or the philosophy of the organization you work for, each person is ultimately responsible for her own spiritual well-being.

Part of working for somebody else is that you must be accountable. Even so, it's important to set realistic goals, remembering to leave enough time for the flow and dance of life to take over. If you just let things happen, rather than pushing them into a time slot, things will flow easily. More will be accomplished with less stress and wear and tear on your body and your soul.

Many women at the top of organizations have to face so many obstacles their heads are ringing from butting up against the proverbial wall. But don't give up — you can make a difference. Be prepared to hit obstacles but instead of crashing up against them, embrace the moment and move with it. Keep your heart open for the best outcome, and attract the right people to help you with what you need. When you are aligned with your purpose and values, you have a great advantage that will serve everyone.

IN RESPONSE TO THE WORKPLACE DEMISE FACING THE FEMININE HEART, many women are choosing to start their own business. Entrepreneurship gives them the flexibility they need to have balance and to express their innermost hearts' desire. However, this is not possible for everyone.

If you are currently in a situation that does not satisfy your values and desires, take responsibility for yourself to create the best situation you can within your own sphere of influence.

If you must work in a totally unnatural environment, get outside on your lunch break or anytime during the day. Fifteen minutes of fresh air and sunshine can do wonders for your mind and body. You alone must make this happen. No one is going to tell you to do it. Take a few minutes on your coffee or lunch break to be alone and go inside to connect with Spirit. You will return to your desk feeling refreshed and ready to take on whatever or whoever passes by your desk.

The more strongly you identify with your Feminine Heart, the more sensitive you are to your physical environment. Make the effort to make your workspace a place that expresses your soul. Bring in personal items that help keep your heart open – photos of people you love, real plants or flowers, anything that reminds you of nature. Things that remind you of a life outside of those walls will help restore your Spirit.

Musings & Blessings

WHAT ACTIVITIES BRING YOU THE MOST JOY? What are you doing when you feel the most alive? When do you find that time flies by because you are so in the moment you lose track of the passing minutes?

These are clues that will point you toward your purpose and calling. If what you are doing is a natural expression of your feminine destiny, you will never have to "work" for a living. You will be living for your work. This is sharing our greatest gifts, a blessing to the world.

Breathe in all the love that you are and all that you have to offer. Exhale, sharing that love with others. Breathe in more love.

We make a living by what we get. We make a life by what we give.
— SIR WINSTON CHURCHILL —

Our Soul's Purpose

My Darling Feminine Heart:

Sometimes I get so frustrated
when I feel that I am not living
to my full potential.
I have been given gifts
that are meant to be shared.
If I should die before I wake,
it would be a travesty
that I never gave all that I had.
Thank you, Goddess,
for giving me a special purpose
and the wisdom to express it.

It's not doing what you like that's important — it's liking what you do.
– ERIC BUTTERWORTH –

LOOK BEYOND WHAT YOU DO FOR A LIVING AND ASK, "Why am I here?" The answer is, "to create and fulfill your soul purpose."

"What is my soul purpose?" you may ask.

Janet Amare, in her book *Soul Purpose*, says she uses the term Soul Purpose to mean the life path that aligns you with your highest potential for happiness, fulfillment and joy. If you are expressing some of your gifts at work, or working with people who share a common vision of creating value for others, then you are indeed blessed.

When we look at our lives from that deep place of knowing, and we start living in that place, we transform. When we follow that inner voice, magic happens. Unexpected things show up as opportunities, and those opportunities take us closer to the full expression of our Highest Self, our truth. At some point we start living for ourselves, not for what others think we should be doing. At that point, we begin to create a purposeful legacy. It isn't so important what the legacy is, but rather that we leave something worthwhile behind after we have ceased to physically exist.

For years I delivered a workshop called "Finding Your Passion" to clients who had lost their jobs and were forced to look at their next career step. Invariably the workshop participants would start with what they wanted now, rather than with what they wanted to leave behind. I would have to explain that finding what they wanted to leave behind would give them meaning and purpose now.

Many people have forgotten what is important to them. After years of going around and around on the proverbial treadmill, we become dulled to the routine of our lives, not giving much thought to the possibility of a passion-filled life.

Ask yourself this: "What is missing on the planet today? What really bothers me about what is happening in the world?" Create a vision of how you would like it to be, and then find a way to contribute to that greater good.

M Y PARENTS DIVORCED WHEN my youngest sister finished high school, dutifully waiting until the youngest of their four daughters was out of the nest. Growing up watching our parents' relationship, the four of us had little positive modeling for our own marriages. We've all been divorced — at least once.

My teenage son is the by-product of a broken marriage. I left my husband when my son was 18 months old. It was not a healthy situation for any of us. When he was four years old, I asked him what he wanted Santa to bring him for Christmas.

"More than anything I want Mommy and Daddy to be together," he said pleadingly. It broke my heart. That was not something I could give him. I felt powerless. I felt that I had let him down. I had. As parents we always want what's best for the people we care most about.

Looking around, I see so many people affected by the tragedies of divorce. Innocent children are always affected by the turmoil and upset that occurs when a relationship falls apart to such an extent that the parents can no longer live together peacefully. This impacts children on so many levels. My heart goes out to these little ones. The messages I see our next generation receiving about love and life with the opposite sex are very disheartening to me. I became passionate about making a contribution in this area. I felt that I could lessen the needless pain that comes from broken relationships and broken hearts. I looked for ways to passionately express my vision of the kind of world that I want for our children's children.

If we have peace in our homes, that energy will extend into our communities. Ultimately, it will increase the loving energy on our planet.

My vision is of a peaceful world, where children witness a deep love and respect between men and women. This is the driving force behind my mission to help people discover their highest purpose, allowing them to consciously choose and maintain loving relationships that will nurture and guide future generations. It is my dream that our children will model the loving relationships between their parents and other adults, and that they will be empowered to create positive, loving and respectful relationships with the opposite sex when they are adults.

If we have peace in our homes, that energy will extend into our communities. Ultimately, it will increase the loving energy on our planet.

I do this by speaking to groups, by counseling and by writing. I feel my work is important and I am passionate about it, so it doesn't feel like work. It is an extension of who I am.

WHAT GETS YOU OUT OF BED EACH MORNING? Is your purpose compelling enough to keep you going when life gets rough? What do you have to offer life? At the end of each day, do you feel that you've contributed the best of who you are?

If you've forgotten your life purpose, a good way to remember is to start at the end of your life. Visualize the day of your funeral. Close your eyes. What do you see? Look at the surroundings. Who is there? What are they doing? Somebody is reading your eulogy. What does it say about your life? What have you done that has left a mark? How have you made a difference to others, now that you have passed on to the other side?

This is a good place to start planning your life direction. Are things today moving you in the direction of what you want to leave behind? If not, start making decisions that will move you toward the life you want to live and the one you will someday leave.

As you journey through your days, stopping often and just breathing, be aware of the underlying motivation behind your actions and your intentions. Why do you do the things you do? Is it for selfish, manipulative or fearful reasons? Is it for honest service with integrity? Is what you are doing moving you toward what you want to be?

Maybe you do not know the answers to these questions. Perhaps your activity lacks purpose. This is a great way to enhance awareness and be more conscious. Being aware of your intentions is fundamental to seeing the beauty manifest in your world.

Dr. Wayne Dyer has written a wonderful book, *The Power of Intention*, which focuses on living out of intention to create a powerful life. He says, "This field of intent can't be described with words, for the words emanate from the field, just as do the questions. That placeless place is intention, and it handles everything for us."

I<small>N THE EARLY</small> 1990s I was working as a management consultant designing and delivering workshops to some of America's largest corporations. With my background in healing, massage therapy and psychology, I was aware of the many day-to-day stressors in the workplace.

I saw a lot of slaughtering in the corporate world. One of my responsibilities was to assist senior managers in large corporations get rid of deadwood — people who were detracting from the financial bottom line. I was the axeman, so to speak. I went into a company and sat down with managers of the affected departments to discuss any issues that could be expected as they told the affected staff members that their services would no longer be needed. People's lives were being thrown into turmoil. The companies called it downsizing, or "rightsizing," as it came to be known.

After being quickly introduced to the departing staff person behind closed doors, I left with the victim usually in tears (of devastation or joy — everyone in those days was given a sack of cash to help make the transition easier). During the ensuing months or years that I worked with these people, I came to know them as people. The higher the positions they had held, the more support they received. I supported them while they rode a roller coaster of emotions, having had the twin rugs of financial security and personal identity pulled out from beneath their feet.

At one point I designed a stress management workshop for a couple of our major clients. One of the exercises required participants to stand behind a seated colleague with their hands on the colleague's shoulders. With my experience in healing, I knew that simply touching a distressed person — the mere presence of another person's energy — would help alleviate a variety of conditions caused by stress.

When I presented this workshop internally at our company, the senior partner was adamant. "We can't have people touching each other in our workshops or we'll have sexual harassment problems," he told me firmly.

At that point I knew the truth of who I was. I realized what my greatest gifts were. I knew that in this particular corporate environment I would be limited in my ability to make a difference. I knew that I would have to move on, to contribute in other ways if I was to be congruent with my Feminine Heart.

The most fulfilled people are those who can express their truth in their work. The Feminine Heart knows her greatest gifts. It is a blessing when your work allows you to express those gifts as part of your regular workday.

Musings & Blessings

HOW DO YOU EXPRESS YOUR PURPOSE? Are you waiting for *someday* to express it? For that special someone? For when you have lost 10 pounds, or finished that romance novel? For after you get divorced? As each day passes you lose the chance to get the most juice from it, and when it is gone, it's gone forever.

Do you live your days as though they are numbered? Each day is an opportunity to share your purpose and your love. If you ignore this opportunity, you are actually snuffing out your radiance! Take a moment to think about what you want to be known for. What legacy do you want to leave behind, after your physical body has left the planet?

If you start with the end in mind, it is much easier to think about what has to be done now to move in that direction. Create a vision that calls deeply upon your Spirit. Ask for guidance and it will be given you. Listen to the message that

comes your way, without being attached to how the message is delivered. Look for the message in clouds, listen to songs, feel the racing of your heart as you move closer to your life's destiny. When you have an open heart, all will be delivered to you. Be ready and stay open.

Breathe in light … pure light. Focussing on that light, exhale all that love. Breathe in again … .

The great thing in the world is not so much where we stand,
as in what direction we are moving.
— OLIVER WENDELL HOLMES —

Everyday Ecstasy

My Darling Feminine Heart:

The tears of joy
don't grace my face
as often as I wish.
They do come; usually when I am empty
and feel little
but your love.
The fullness of it
gushes out of me.
Even my heart feels refreshed.
Thank you, Goddess, for the joy of ecstasy
as an everyday experience.

There is no value in life except what you choose to place upon it
and no happiness in any place except what you bring to it yourself.
– HENRY DAVID THOREAU –

THE HAPPIEST WOMEN ARE THOSE WHO HAVE THE WISDOM to know that they are co-creators of their life experiences. They recognize the presence in themselves of a loving and creative Spirit. They have learned not just to pray, but to acknowledge the constant presence of their Higher Selves. They have awakened their hearts to embrace the power of Spirit as part of their everyday activities, creating the experience of daily ecstasy.

Light workers have a personal stake in the transformation of human consciousness, as we work to dispel fear with our openhearted love. We begin with ourselves, recognizing our cravings as a call from above aching to be expressed and shared with others. This is the gift that keeps on giving, because love begets love.

When women hit middle age, their bodies cannot hide their emotions any longer. If a woman lived most of her life with her heart shut down, her feminine essence starts to exhibit a variety of physiological and psychological problems.

C URRENT RESEARCH CASUALLY REPORTS DEPRESSION, anxiety and unexplained sadness as normal parts of living.

Unfortunately, these feelings and emotions continue to pop up until we release the past and forgive our transgressors. Until that time, however, if we continue to keep our hearts closed, we will suffer. The amount of antidepressants and mood-altering drugs given out by the medical profession indicates that many people have shut down to the point where they can no longer experience the joy of life. These are the automatons of our age, not feeling deeply about anything, simply existing on the surface without feeling their hearts.

This phenomenon affects both men and women, but the repercussions of the feminine not experiencing and expressing her heart affects everyone in her life — her family, friends, colleagues and children. Nobody gets to benefit from her radiance. No one gets to benefit from the healing powers of her Feminine Heart when it is closed.

The more dense the wrapping around the Feminine Heart, the less radiant she appears to be to others. If a woman is filled with fear instead of love, her light is replaced by darkness. Other people, children and animals are sensitive enough to pick up on that energy. If she has a hidden agenda when meeting with a business client, or if she bought something she doesn't want her husband to see, she will relate differently to the client or to her husband — out of fear instead of love.

The health and happiness of the Feminine Heart sets the tone for the well-being of the family. She is the nucleus, feeding all who live and work around her. It is vital that she takes care of her own health and state of mind, so that her family members receive the care and attention that they need to thrive.

How you are feeling affects how others in your life are feeling. You cannot separate yourself from the members of your family. Families are symbiotic structures. Family members look to the Feminine Heart as the emotional barometer of what to expect — every day, every week and every month.

I T IS EASY TO UNDERSTAND WHY IN MANY INDIGENOUS CULTURES, women spent time away from family duties while they were "on their moon." Not only was it a time of cleansing and creativity for the women, it was a time of heightened energy and power that influenced all members of the family. If not honored as a time of special creativity, the powerfully charged emotional energy that ensued could often be destructive to the equilibrium within the family.

Just as the moon goes through a full cycle every 28 days, so follows a woman's reproductive cycle. In our modern culture, many women have become removed from the natural cycles of life. Unlike cultures living close to the earth, many women today are unaware of how the gravitational pull of the moon affects what is happening within their bodies.

I started to chart my periods while still in high school and was astounded to discover that the onset of my periods coincided with the onset of the full moon. There were some years when my cycle shifted and the onset of my period coincided with the start of a new moon. Indigenous cultures are aware of this phenomenon and that is why they refer to a woman's menstrual cycle as her "moon cycle."

Growing up with four other women — my mother and three sisters — we were very much in tune with each other's cycles. Virtually every month, all of us would have our period at the same time. Women who live in close proximity with other women experience this. Women who live together bleed together when their bodies are left to function naturally — without the use of birth control pills or hormones. The intricacies of the menstrual cycle while subtle are incredibly powerful.

In our fast-paced, modern world, most women don't take time during their menstrual cycles to acknowledge that something profound is taking place within their bodies. They don't make the effort to look inward, become quiet in their center, and give thanks for one of life's sacred mysteries. Most women have both work and family responsibilities and feel their daily routines must continue uninterrupted. Consequently, the natural occurrence of a monthly menstrual cycle is seen as a great inconvenience to modern life.

Pharmaceutical companies have fully exploited the dilemmas faced by women today and have created drugs that can alter when a woman gets her period, or stop her from having a period at all. The advantages, they suggest, are that women have more choices — to pursue any sort of activity, go on a vacation, or plan their wedding and honeymoon — all without the inconvenience of having these things coincide with an unwanted menstrual cycle. If women so choose, they can also eliminate their monthly cycle of hormonal change altogether.

In our Western culture we have denigrated this important time of creative regeneration as nothing more than a nuisance. Rather than embracing these aspects of our femininity as a gift, and using this time to delve deeper into our feminine emotions and psyche, some women would rather get rid of their periods altogether.

As a culture, we are distancing ourselves from the natural essence of what it means to be a woman. Embrace your emotions. Be moved by them. Allow them to take you places in your body, mind and spirit that you could never access if you completely shut off this flow of divine creative energy. The gift of power and wisdom that you have access to during this time of the month can be harnessed to bring insights and clarification about the goings-on in your world. Your dreams are more vivid, your creative endeavors more fully expressed, and your tears bigger. The feminine creative essence is expressing itself most fully during this time.

While working with Native American healers, I learned that when the wives were on their "moon cycles" they were relieved of all their worldly duties. The women spent time by themselves, following their creative desires, resting, or connecting with themselves and their power. At the end of their cycle, refreshed, they would bring renewed energy back to the family.

As a culture, we are distancing ourselves from the natural essence of what it means to be a woman.

The power these women had during their menstrual cycle was honored and revered. "My wife's emotional power was 20 times stronger than mine while she was on her moon," one native healer told me. That is why women were not allowed into the sweat lodges during this time — their power could affect the experience of others during this time of spiritual cleansing.

This sounded like a complete luxury to me, a single mother with no other family members in the city where I lived. For my sake, and the sake of my son, I could not check out of my worldly duties every month during my period! I had to continue doing what I did every other day of the month, even though my chores did feel more onerous and my tears came more easily.

I learned to make some amendments, however. I realized the importance of connecting with my feminine energy, and took extra care to look after myself in ways that I sometimes didn't bother with during the rest of the month. The moon cycle is a time to connect with others, reaching out to express love and to receive love. So I would call a friend, or get together with someone special for a walk and talk. In the evenings, rather than having a quick shower I would linger in the bath for longer than necessary. I made sure to scent the water with something special, and when I got out I applied a favorite perfume, scented lotion or an aromatherapy spray, treating myself to the smells that made me feel the most womanly — alive, sensual and feminine. Then I would dress myself in something feminine that was usually bypassed in my closet at other times of the month.

Embrace those aspects that make you distinct from the masculine. Be proud of the differences that you offer the other half of humanity and share that polarity so that the masculine can more fully feel his sexual essence. This is the gift you have to offer the world... the light of your feminine sexual essence. This is the path to everyday ecstasy.

Musings & Blessings

NOTICE YOUR DREAMS DURING YOUR CYCLE. They may become vivid. Write them down if you are so inspired, so that you may reflect back at a later date after you've had time and space to let things unfold naturally. The cleansing of your body in preparation for the release of a new egg is a creative process that affects your mind and spirit as well as your body.

This is the time of the month to take a different approach to the usual way of doing things. Let go. Have fun. Honor the timeless feminine Spirit that exists in women everywhere.

As you do what it is the heavens require, you shall receive pieces of yourself.
— RAY THOMPSON —

Radiant Health

My Darling Feminine Heart:

When I take care of you
to the best of my ability
you take care of me.
When my spirit is nurtured
my emotions are blessings
and my body is vital and strong.
When I honor my body's needs
my mind is calm
and my spirit is bright.
Thank you, Goddess, for the gift of radiant health.

Without health, you have nothing.
– Old English Saying –

EVERYBODY HAS HEARD THIS SAYING AT SOME POINT IN THEIR LIVES. Usually, it is only when we have lost our health that the saying hits home. Even love and money lose their value when you do not have radiant health to enjoy the bounties of life.

Your body knows what it likes. When it's happy, it feels good. Your body is the source of your vitality, your motivation, your inspiration, your enthusiasm and, most importantly, your intuition. If you are venturing into a new activity, it is best to get that part of you — your all-important intuition — onside.

Are you aware of your body's wisdom? Our bodies usually know us better than our minds do. If you have a decision to make, consult your body before making a final choice. Reflect on an option before you, and then pay attention to your body. Are you breathing deeply or barely at all? Are your muscles tense or relaxed? Is your energy blocked, or flowing freely?

You can do many things to help ensure continuing good health. One of the most important is to drink lots and lots of pure water. The brain is approximately 83 per cent water, and a dehydrated brain cannot think or process information easily. Studies show that drinking pure, living water can greatly improve your health and mental clarity as well as enhance your creativity and increase your lifespan.

Practising yoga helps stretch all the body structures. It relaxes the internal organs and releases stress. While focusing on the well-being of the body and going through the various movements, circulation is increased, tension is released and the entire body becomes relaxed and balanced.

Keeping a dream journal is an excellent way to see what emotional residue lingers in your body and mind. As discussed in The Gift of Intuition, the process of writing down your dreams upon awakening is an excellent way to capture situations held in the subconscious mind that affect your physical body.

Find a way to still your babbling mind and listen to your deeper wisdom. Meditation is a time-honored way to recognize emotional weakness in your body and to become conscious of it in a detached way. Meditation helps to release stressors in the body, so that you can adopt new emotional patterns of behavior. (See The Power of Prayer and Meditation on pages 220 – 222.)

Humor is an excellent tool for reducing stress and negative emotions. This has been my own personal quest — to increase the amount of laughter in my life. It costs nothing, takes no time and has immense value. Norman Cousins, in the book Anatomy of an Illness, documents how potent laughter can be in healing the mind and body. As the saying goes, there is no medicine better than laughter!

SEVERAL YEARS AGO, I was physically and emotionally exhausted. Much to my dismay, I came down with mononucleosis. Not knowing much about mono I started researching it, talking to the most knowledgeable people in the field. Western medical practitioners, naturopaths and healers from the Eastern healing traditions agree that many diseases are caused by stress that has compromised our immune systems.

Losing my health and vitality to mononucleosis was a real physical setback, but not nearly as transformational as the emotional and spiritual components of my illness. Realizing that good health is indeed one of life's greatest blessings, to get my health back on track I slowed down, cleansed my body, mind and Spirit, and approached life at a different pace. This was what I needed to restore my health and vitality.

Sometimes blessings come when we lose our health. We are required to make a change. The change must start from within before it can manifest outwardly in our physical bodies. As we go inside and listen to the messages from our Higher Selves, our questions will be answered as to what changes we must make. Have faith in the message. If you have not yet lost your health, don't wait until you are in your 40s or 50s and collapse in a heap because your body can't take anymore.

The regular practice of deep, relaxed breathing can help create vitality and health by balancing the mind, body and emotions. The enlightened woman knows how important breathing is for optimal health and well-being. Conscious breathing can also help with overeating problems. Overeating is often a need of the mind and emotions, more than a need of the stomach. Deep breathing helps to reduce the need to overeat by balancing the metabolism and calming the mind.

How we breathe can affect how others around us will react. I often use my breath to alter a situation. While giving deep massages and healing, I protected myself by focusing on bringing in white light while breathing deeply — filling my lungs with the visual of the clear, white light of Spirit. I did this to raise my energy field and protect me from the energy being released by the client. Exhaling, I would let go of anything that was not clean and pure — any negative thought or feeling that I was holding inside.

Everything has a cost. If you have poor breathing habits developed in childhood or from living a sedentary life, your breathing is shallow and superficial. This kind of breathing deprives the body of prana (the vital life force) and the oxygen that feeds the body. Years of improper breathing will result in premature aging and a noticeable deterioration in health. In fact, all the functions of the body, voluntary and involuntary, from our organs to our mental functioning, are governed by prana.

How we breathe can affect our emotions, as well as our physical and mental state. Notice how you breathe when you are afraid or very angry. When you learn to be aware of your breathing you can maintain a relaxed breathing pattern when you are tense, sending a very different message to your nervous system. If you maintain a deep and relaxed rhythm in your breathing, your emotions will not leave their energy-draining mark of stress on your body and mind. Usually, our emotions go unnoticed until they become so overpowering that we have difficulty letting them flow through us. We become slaves to them.

Nobel prizewinner Dr. Candace Pert is an internationally recognized pharmacologist who has undertaken extensive research on the role of emotions and the mind-body connection. In her book, *Molecules of Emotion: Why You Feel the Way You Feel*, Dr. Pert explains how intrinsically our health is affected by our thoughts, feelings and emotions.

In her work she describes someone we all know — the woman who could be described as the SuperMom. These women are bright, capable, type-A achievers with post-secondary educations. After university, SuperMom met the right guy, started a home, got pregnant and had 2.3 kids. She stayed at home making sure everything was perfect around the house until the kids were in school, and now she wants to enter the workforce. Because she is SuperMom, she is not content in some fluffy little part-time job, but wants to run her own business or take an executive position doing a full day's work while still being a perfect mother, retaining her figure, and giving two dinner parties a week. All this she does perfectly, Martha Stewart style.

Does this scenario remind you of anybody you know? Do you ever find yourself racing through your days as though a big prize is waiting at the finish line? Although we may get accolades for all our *doing*, we lose out on the journey. We get to the end of the race but forget why we entered in the first place. The prize is not what we had anticipated. Yes, the strokes of accomplishment feel good. But if in the process we lose the essence of ourselves or our health, we have actually lost the only prize worth racing for.

When we lose our health and vitality, we have little to offer others. Coping becomes a way of life. Without vibrant health, the light of our feminine radiance is barely visible, if it shines at all. We cannot be of service to others if we do not take care of ourselves. Health is one of our most precious commodities. Guard it like a priceless treasure. Our thoughts, feelings and emotions play a huge role in our physical well-being. Embracing the wisdom of Spirit gives us the strength and courage to do those things that will make the biggest difference in our lives and the lives of others, while retaining radiant health.

Musings & Blessings

How do you feel when you remember to breathe in pure, white light and to exhale any dark or negative thoughts or feelings?

You can also do this when you are feeling sluggish or burdened by life. It will not only put a spring back in your step, but it will make you feel about 10 pounds lighter — something that will put you in a different frame of mind. Try deep, relaxing breathing the next time you are feeling tense or stressed out and see if it helps calm your nerves. Using prayer and meditation can also help you relax. I know it works for me.

Breathe in vibrant and radiant health. Giving thanks for life, exhale. Breathe in love.

The time to relax is when you don't have the time for it.
— SIDNEY J. HARRIS —

The Power of Prayer & Meditation

My Darling Feminine Heart:

When I allow myself
to go away with you
you never disappoint.
Fleeting moments or regular visits
always gift me deeply.
When we depart,
I am left with a stronger sense
of my divine essence
than I was aware of
before I joined you in reverence.
Thank you, Goddess, for gently holding my Spirit
during our quiet and loving visits.

*Nowhere can you retire with more quietness or more freedom
than within your own spirit — constantly give yourself to this retreat,
and renew yourself.*
– MARCUS AURELIUS ANTONINUS –

IF YOU ARE HAVING TROUBLE CONNECTING to that all-knowing inner voice, try listening during the quiet of prayer and meditation. This can be done anywhere, at any time. If it is available, a room with a door closed to external busy-ness makes it that much easier. Lowering the lights and lighting a candle may help eliminate distractions. It doesn't take much to become distracted. Aromatherapy and the essential oils of lavender or ylang-ylang can help relax you and connect you with your senses. You may have to post a little Do Not

Disturb sign, making sure that your family members or colleagues at work understand and respect your wishes.

The more feminine your essence, the more difficult it will be to stay focused for long periods of time. The feminine desire is to flow and to move with what is going on in the moment. A number of things will help you to stay in your body and be present to the now. Breathing deeply helps to get centered and be present in your body. Breathe fully from the diaphragm, feeling the love and wisdom that is in and around you. Upon exhaling, relax your body and release any thoughts, doubts or fears that don't support the truth of who you know yourself to be. Continue this slow, rhythmical breathing until you feel a sense of calm, quiet and peace.

Trust any messages that come during this period of quiet reflection. They are there for a reason. They may be old thoughts from yesterday or new thoughts about the future. Let these thoughts pass through your mind like a stream flowing around the hard, jagged rocks of a river. These thoughts are the residue of a busy mind. Real peace begins once the thoughts have made their journey downstream and all that is left is still water, quiet and deep. It is in the depth of this solitude that we find ourselves.

Breathe deeply, focus your energy inward, and ask your inner Spirit to guide you. Breathe out deeply, letting go of anything that does not feel like love. Access those places of denseness in your body (we all hold tension in different places) and exhale, releasing any tightness or discomfort. Clear yourself, and move your energy into your body. Continue breathing in light and exhaling anything that does not feel like love.

Continue several times until you feel calm, balanced and connected with your Source. This works wonders even if you just do it a couple of times quickly before you yell at your kids, or lose it at the driver who just cut you off. Just release, and let it go. When this process becomes habit, you will be able to get to that balanced place much more quickly.

Use this process before you go into meditation, as it will energize your body. Breathing more deeply and fully deepens any moment.

Musings & Blessings

To purify your heart, become aware of the times that you give thanks throughout the day. Popular wisdom has it that we should go to bed at night giving thanks for at least five things that happened during the day. It is a positive practice, especially for those bad days when it feels like there is little to be thankful for.

If, however, you can practice giving thanks in the moment, and you can then learn how to extend those moments, your heart will cleanse itself and become pure love. What do you have to lose? Try counting all the things you have to be grateful for instead of calories. The impact on your mind *and* body will be amazing.

Breathe in a deep connection with your Creator. Exhale, with heartfelt gratitude. Breathe in love. You are one with God.

The wish to pray is a prayer in itself.
— GEORGES BENANOS —

Unselfish Solitude

My Darling Feminine Heart:

My apologies for being away
for so long.
Sometimes I can't feel or hear you
the din of life is so loud.
Then I know it's time to come home to you.
I take myself back to that place
where you wait.
You are always there waiting.
I just don't see you unless I come on my own.
And once there
I am never alone.
Thank you, Goddess, for being with me in all ways.

I have never found the companion that was so companionable as solitude.
— HENRY DAVID THOREAU —

AT HER CORE, the Feminine Heart is concerned with the quality of her personal relationships. Our relationships are paramount to us. With a focus on giving and receiving love, solitude sounds like a death sentence.

When we find that we have been giving continuously to others, at home and at work, we sometimes feel flattened because we haven't taken the time to give back to ourselves. It is uncommon for our spouses, children or friends to suggest, "Why don't you get away and spend some time by yourself?" In fact, they may feel threatened by the fact that we want to get away and spend time without them. Perhaps they feel neglected or unloved — that we'd rather spend time alone than with them.

As much as we care for our loved ones, we know that we must look after ourselves too, and sometimes that means going it alone. Nothing soothes the rough edges of our weary thoughts like time away by ourselves. This is a gift we must give to ourselves, so that we can give the best of our gifts to others. Sometimes the best way to become renewed is to remove ourselves from the daily routine. Being out in nature, alone, is one of the best remedies for a heavy Feminine Heart.

Only when we can truly be comfortable with ourselves and by ourselves, can we really be there for others. During these times we get a rare chance to be with our own thoughts, and to commune with our Higher Selves. Spirit speaks most loudly when we are in the quiet of our minds.

The great masters from every tradition have stressed the importance of making time daily for solitude. If our journey in life calls us to become more of who we are, then we need to set aside some free time each day to explore our inner landscape, and to uncover our passion.

We all have places that resonate more deeply for us than others. Wherever it is, try to go there whenever possible to renew yourself. It may be the mountains, the ocean, the desert or the forest. Often, the place where as children we fell deeply in love with our Spirit still resonates in our soul.

AT TIMES WHILE WRITING THIS BOOK I just had to get away so I could hear the message I was being asked to share. I would pack up my writing materials and head off to Northern Saskatchewan, to an old log cottage I love. Driving north through the tabletop landscape and the vast spaciousness of blue prairie skies, finally I arrive at Waskesiu Lake. I spent many happy days here as a child, listening to the whisper of wind through pine and birch, and the lonely wailing of the loon.

Now, sitting by myself overlooking the lake gives me such a sense of peace and satisfaction. I feel my batteries being recharged. Alone in nature, away from the hustle of the big city, this is where I live my *real* life. It is the place where I can actually hear my own voice. It is here, in solitude, that I feel comforted and restored. Here I take a vacation with myself. Solitude is a gift of love that I give to me.

My family doesn't fully appreciate my need to be alone. My mother lives about an hour from this lake, and she is often puzzled about my need to travel so far just to sit by myself, to think and to write. Sometimes I don't get a whole lot of work done. The joy and peace that I experience is so beautiful that I don't want to have to do anything. I would rather just sit and be. Here, without the endless phone calls, demands of work and distractions of life, I can easily connect with my Feminine Heart. The loon calls, and my heart sings. I am at home with my beloved.

In these moments of aloneness, we connect with Spirit. During this time, we are strengthening our relationship with ourselves and with our Creator. We are usually so busy that we don't take the time to be quiet. We don't know how to just listen to that quiet voice, the voice that guides and directs when we follow our heart.

Every time I leave my favorite place of solitude, I feel a renewed sense of myself. I like this calm and peaceful person so much more than I like my usual harried and frantic self. It takes conscious effort to retain that Zen-like attitude throughout the daily marathon. But with practice, a few simple deep breaths will take us back to that place of solitude — the place that heals and nurtures.

In our solitude, we can hear our Higher Selves reminding us of the truth and beauty that we are. This is such an important message. But if we don't stop to listen, the message gets lost in the chatter and distractions of daily life.

We don't have to wander away from home to be alone, although it certainly does make it easier. The lure of the phone, fax and email is so compelling that many of us find it almost impossible to resist the temptation of technology when it beckons. It takes discipline and intention to be in our homes but able to disconnect in such a way that we are truly alone. With so many responsibilities and obligations, most of us haven't heard that still and quiet inner voice for a long time. Sometimes we don't even recognize it calling out to us.

Musings & Blessings

WHEN IS THE LAST TIME YOU SPENT ANY AMOUNT OF TIME ALONE? For many women with families, time alone is an almost impossible luxury. It can be accomplished, however, if you take mini-solitude breaks. The consistency of taking time daily to pray or to meditate is helpful, because our Soul knows that it will get fed that day.

If you feel that you already have too much to do, ask yourself, "What activity can I give up today, so that I can have some time alone with my beloved Feminine Heart?" The answer will come quickly.

How often do you get out in nature? Nature heals the Feminine Heart. In nature, we tune in to all of life. If you live or work in a masculine environment for most of your day, the following exercise will be useful. When I am in the beauty and solitude of nature I tend to keep my eyes open while doing this exercise, but in the city you may find it easier to keep your eyes closed.

Focus on your breathing, taking in the air from deep within. Continue breathing, deeply taking in all of nature. Feel the pure mist of a mountain stream, or the fresh air rising from a pine and moss forest passing over your nostrils. As you exhale, let go of any pain or darkness that you can feel. Continue breathing, taking in the blessing of Mother Earth. Give thanks for her gifts. Listen for her response. When you hear what she has to say, give thanks and go in peace.

Breathe in love. Exhale any sadness or loneliness. Breathe in the connectedness with all life.

When we cannot find contentment in ourselves,
it is useless to seek it elsewhere.
– Francois de La Rochefoucauld –

Grace & Gratitude

My Darling Feminine Heart:

My love for you is strong
yet I know you feel me waver.
During the dark hours of life
that challenge my gracious heart
I must find the strength to see the gift
each challenge offers.
When I go inside and feel your greatness
imprinted within my heart,
I am once again with you.
It is the grace of your love
that offers the lessons I need
to become more fully who I am
In deep gratitude I give thanks, dear Goddess,
for all that I am given.

The fuel for a blissful life is gratitude.
— GERALD G. JAMPOLSKY —

THE GRACIOUSNESS OF OUR HEARTS and the desire to give love and receive love is innate in women. Gratitude is our eternal thankfulness in our ability to partake in this life.

Although gratitude is natural, without conscious effort it does not become a part of our daily affairs. If we are constantly running around like chickens with our heads cut off, it may be difficult to incorporate gratitude as part of our daily rituals, like brushing our teeth. Over time, however, and with awareness, we can make gratitude a part of our lives. Grace is the natural expression of a life lived in gratitude.

Currently, a good part of my year is spent in Calgary, a young, vibrant city rich in technology and the spoils of the oil and gas industry. It is very masculine in its energy. I find myself running to and fro, feeling stressed for no apparent reason. Some days, unless I start my day with a morning meditation or prayer, it is not until I tuck my son into bed at night that I feel grace in my heart.

It takes conscious effort to slow down enough to realize where the wonder and grace of life exists. It is all around us, but we must slow down enough to be aware of it, and be to be grateful for the life we have.

Take the example of eating. We have to eat. Throughout each day we put hundreds of things into our mouths without much thought. But stop! When we go though the motions of eating with an attitude of gratitude, we are not just eating for survival. True, we are nourishing our bodies, but our Spirits are also being fed with the blessing of gratitude. No matter how humble our offerings, when we eat with heartfelt gratitude even the simplest of fare becomes divine.

Before putting your feet on the floor in the morning, take a moment and give thanks for the opportunity of having another day on this planet. At the end of the day, before drifting off into dreamland, mentally go over your day and feel gratitude for all the goodness that crossed your path.

Teaching children to give thanks at an early age gives them a lifetime of seeing blessings at every turn. This can only give them a sense of strength and calm as they face their challenges in the journey through life.

I read an interview with Masaru Emoto, the Japanese scientist who has done extensive research on how water can be infused with different vibrational qualities. His book, *The Hidden Messages in Water*, displays spectacular photos of water molecules infused with different vibrations using particular words and phrases demonstrating his theories.

He believes that the word love in combination with the word gratitude contains amazing healing properties. "Just one of these is not enough. Love needs to be based in gratitude and gratitude needs to be based in love," he states.

Our bodies are composed of water similar to ocean water. The salt crystals contained in this water vibrate at ever-changing frequencies. Our emotional center stems from our open heart, which puts out frequencies that are 10 times

Mixing Love with Gratitude

The miracle of changed consciousness
comes from placing the attention
above the difficulties of the day.
With deep gratitude
comes true humility,
a key to the fountain of youth.
Gratitude lights the way to enthusiasm.
Enthusiasm clears the path to love.
Love is the key to freedom.
— SANDY PARIS —

the power of the frequencies of our brains. In other words, our emotional state changes the chemical composition of the water in our bodies. Perhaps that's why our happy tears taste differently than tears falling from sadness.

When we open our hearts to love with gratitude, our bodies become stronger and our minds become serene. Our physical body vibrates at a higher frequency, allowing healing to occur.

HAWAII IS A FEMININE PLACE, full of vibrant beauty and lush surroundings. It is difficult not to feel grateful for life when surrounded by such overt beauty. When I lived there, I embraced the concept of gratitude with fervor. I discovered how gratitude is the key to living a life of grace.

My friends and I would often marvel at how our intentions would manifest, making things we desired come true. We came to call this phenomenon "Mother Maui's magic." Actually it was the grace of Spirit, the force that lives and breathes in everything. When we become aware of its presence, it is very powerful. I made a conscious effort to see the grace and magic in everything.

Every night, just before sunset, I would stand behind our house in Maui Meadows overlooking the ocean and give thanks for the day. Nothing was too insignificant to be part of my gratitude-filled prayers. Sometimes it would be a simple thing, like giving thanks for the beautiful flowers in our backyard, or for the sincere smile from the elderly Japanese gentleman at the tofu factory that I frequented. My friends and I were so attuned to the grace in our lives that life did seem like magic.

GIVING THANKS COMES EASILY when we receive the things our hearts desire most. An attitude of gratitude comes naturally when our life is working and moving in the direction of our dreams.

It is when our challenges are the greatest, the dangers the gravest, and despair the deepest, that the extent of our gratitude is put to the test. This is when the face of grace becomes unrecognizable — unless we have faith that grace and gratitude come in a variety of disguises.

In 1974 I was living on the island of Maui, where I had a baking business. I supplied various retail outlets with goodies made without animal products for the burgeoning vegetarian population. Several of my accounts were located around the island, so twice a week I delivered my baking to these outlets.

I drove an old yellow Volkswagen station wagon. I called it the Banana. One morning, heading up-country for my weekly delivery, the Banana's engine started to overheat. With smoke billowing out of the hood, I thought I had better pull over before something major happened.

This was before cell phones. With no taxi service on the island, hitchhiking was fairly commonplace. The friendly locals often stopped to give hitchhikers a ride. Standing beside the Banana under the hot sun with my thumb out, waiting patiently for a ride back to town, I started to perspire beneath my long, silky, rayon muu muu. Cars whizzed by. I was beginning to feel a little helpless and discouraged. Finally, a bright red truck pulled over. The driver, a stocky man with fiery red wires for hair, didn't say much.

"Get in."

I realized he wasn't going to be much of a conversationalist. A local guy, his hair was bleached from surfing and his stubby hands clenched the steering wheel. I noticed how rough they were. He was probably a laborer, doing something physical for work.

In stony silence he continued driving while I studied his profile. His red eyes had no lashes and reminded me of a goat's eyes, almost evil. I began to feel uncomfortable. Moments later, he turned onto a side road leading into a high field of sugar cane.

"Where are you going?" I asked nervously, trying to remain calm. Because of their denseness, cane fields were notorious places for rape.

"Taking a shortcut to town," he answered, gruffly.

"Would you mind letting me out here?" I asked, my pulse quickening and a shot of fear running through my veins.

Goat man said nothing. He continued driving another mile before stopping. He grabbed my arm, pulling me outside and throwing me onto the front of the truck. I am a large woman and strong, but I was no match for this animal. I was terrified. With the full weight of his body holding me against the warm metal of the truck, he took out a switchblade and a crumpled red handkerchief.

"Please God, don't let this happen to me," I whimpered, frozen in terror. He pressed his body hard into my stomach. A mad dog in heat, he ran his body up and down against mine. It was high noon, and he was sweating. As he pressed into my body I could smell his dirty, wet hair. His smell made me sick. I looked up to the heavens, trembling and shaking with fear.

"Please God, help me!" I whispered, thinking of all the times I should have trusted in God, but didn't. "I promise never to forget you again. I promise to be faithful. I promise!"

Tears started rolling down my cheeks. "Please save me from this man," I begged. "He is in pain, and I am in pain too. Please save me from harm and save this man from doing something that he will forever regret."

The rubbing started to slow. I looked at the animal bracing me and there was a tear rolling down his cheek. He stopped gyrating, and his goat eyes looked deep into me. "You're a good woman. You didn't try to hurt me," he said shakily.

He grabbed my hair and threw me to the side. Dashing into his truck, he tore back down the dusty road. I lay there, sobbing with fear and with relief that I was not further violated.

I was crying for another reason, too. I had felt the grace of God that day. The presence of that grace blessed both of us to such an extent that my assailant no longer felt the need to hurt me.

I walked all the way back into town, crying most of the way. On the outskirts of Wailuku town a historic stone church sits in the shade of a cool coconut grove. It was late afternoon. I hadn't been into a church for some time, but I tugged on the door. There was no one inside. Sitting in quiet solitude in the front pew, my well of tears gushed forth again.

This time, however, they were tears of joy. I had been protected by God's grace, and I was humbled by that fact. I knew that my life would be forever changed. I would never again lose my faith in the power of prayer and the power of love and grace. I gave thanks from the deepest part of my soul. Rarely a day has passed since, when I have not remembered to thank my Creator.

When you are faced with problems and situations that seem insurmountable, remember that a gift awaits. Our tests deepen our faith. With an attitude of gratitude nothing can upset our peace. It is all good. It is all God.

Musings & Blessings

WHEN DO YOU NOTICE THE GRACE OF GOD as a presence in your life? Do you give thanks for its presence? Look at the smallest of miracles that come into your life, and give thanks.

When problems arise, they force us to go inside and see the gift that is there. Once you turn inward and connect with Spirit, you will find the courage to face life's storms. Turn the problem into an opportunity, and be grateful for the learning that occurs.

Breathe in love and light. Give thanks for all of it. Exhaling deeply, spread your gratitude and love. Beathe in more love.

Gratitude makes sense of our past, brings peace for today,
and creates a vision for tomorrow.
– MELODIE BEATTIE –

Together all Things are Possible

My Darling Feminine Heart:

I know I make a difference
when I share my love and my light.
Like a pebble thrown into the pool of humanity
ripples roll where I dive in…
spreading hope of a new possibility.
But ripples aren't enough now.
Mother Earth's demise requires
that our ripples melt together
forming a swell that rises like a mighty wave.
Each of our hearts must dive into the ocean of the future.
Our radiant hearts will work together to create a light so bright
that the pain and darkness creating her suffering
is exposed and transformed.
Alone we can make a difference.
United, the Feminine Heart will transform fear and hatred into love,
war into peace, with enough for all.
Our children's children will see the divine
reflected in the eyes of each other in a new era of love.
Thank you, Goddess, for the opportunity
of gifting humanity to the next level of consciousness.

If ever there comes a time when the women of the world come together
purely and simply for the benefit of mankind,
it will be a force such as the world has never seen.
— MATTHEW ARNOLD —

OPPOSITES ATTRACT. Male and female, yin and yang, the magnetic poles of positive and negative — all are subject to the laws of attraction. On a spiritual level, however, attraction takes the form of a vibration deep within the soul.

The old saying, "birds of a feather flock together," still resonates today. Look at your friends or the people that you feel deeply at home and at peace with. Even within your own blood family, you will vibrate more resonantly with certain family members than with others. Again, it is not about judging the situation, but just being aware of what exists, and who you are being, in the relationship. Spend time and energy with like-minded souls who know their purpose and are willing to accept the responsibility of that knowledge. It is a power unlike any the world has experienced before in history — it is the power of a new era of love.

Feminine Hearts all over the planet are once again embracing their Goddess Spirit. Whether they live in San Francisco or Bombay, they are taking a stand to become a bearer of God's light where darkness prevails. Working together to share this light of love is so powerful, and we are only beginning to see the effects of what we can accomplish.

Make a practice of starting your day by asking your Spirit this question: "How can I share more of who I came to be today that will make a difference in the world?" Don't take this on as if it is simply another item on your to-do list. Set your intention that whatever you undertake is done in the spirit of love. If each Feminine Heart consciously makes an effort to raise the vibration of her own energy, everybody around her will benefit.

You may be surprised at how much love will come back to you. When it does (and it will) breathe it in and let it circulate in your body. As you exhale, share your molecules of air and moisture with the world. If they have been imprinted in your heart with thoughts of love and gratitude, they will fill the spaces they occupy with the healing light that our world so desperately needs.

Look around you. Countless others share a deep concern for the future of our planet. Loving and purposeful men, living their missions by contributing to the greater good of the world desire to connect with enlightened women. Join these men with the intention of healing each other, allowing the highest creative potential of each to unfold. Co-create loving families that emanate peace and a sense of well-being for your children whether or not you have a partner. Join with other like-minded families to create a universal family.

Our children hold the key to the next stage of human evolution. Conscious children know they are the leaders of the future and realize that they are the protectors of Mother Earth. The Feminine Heart must pass over the keys of all our God-given gifts that will bless future generations.

We are powerful beyond measure. As futurist thinker, Malcom Gladwell suggests in *The Tipping Point*, when word of Ya-Ya Sisterhood spread, groups formed on their own — immitating the group described in the book of the same name. The word spread, book-group to book-group, as the author, Reverand Wells toured the country sharing her message. The outcome of these discussion groups were that like-minded people came together to discuss subjects that they were passionate about. The tipping point that will ensure the survival of future generations is now. The time for the love and wisdom of the Feminine Heart has come. By expressing our wisdom and our truth, men and women around the world can create a current so strong that the vortex of love will pull darkness into its depths and transform it with love.

Creating a new era of love is not something that might be nice to do someday when we have time. There is no more time. We must set the intention to use our love, blossoming open the hearts of those whose minds are still mired in darkness and fear. When we share our love with others, they are transformed by it. They can resist, but they can't escape. Everyone needs love. This is a universal truth. Your Feminine Heart has everything it needs to share this message.

Share the light of your radiant Feminine Heart to support others in their purposeful and enlightened endeavors. By working together, sharing our ideas, our time and our resources, we can create a new era of love that will benefit all humankind.

Musings & Blessings

How CAN YOU HELP TO START MOVING the consciousness of our planet toward love? Who could you phone right now and ask to donate something — time, money, used clothing, anything — to others who are not so blessed? As an enlightened woman, you have all the answers within. Take the next step. Voice your wisdom anytime and anywhere you have an opportunity. Share the knowledge of what it will take to heal Mother Earth and help restore her natural beauty. What is your vision for the children of the world? What can you contribute towards making your vision a reality? By taking action and by sharing your vision with other Feminine Hearts, much can be accomplished.

Join hands and hearts with other enlightened souls on this planet. Be brave and be strong. Share your light, hold the intention of the possibility for peace on the planet and watch the unfolding of a new era of love. Give thanks for this possibility. The time is now. Love is all there is.

Breathe in deeply. Feel love's fullness in the depth of your Feminine Heart. Exhale. Share that love and light wherever you go.

Goddess of the light
Goddess of the light
Goddess of the light
UNITE

If the first woman God ever made was strong enough to turn the world upside down, these women together ought to be able to turn it right side up again.
— SOJOURNER TRUTH —

References

WITH A GRATEFUL HEART I WOULD LIKE TO ACKNOWLEDGE THE AUTHORS, whose words I have quoted, for their vision, wisdom and creativity. A concerted effort was made to determine whether any previously published material appearing in this book required permission to reprint. My apologies if there has been an error and a correction will be made in subsequent editions.

Aburdene, P. & Naisbitt, J. (1992). *Megatrends for women.* New York, NY: Villard.

Amare, J. (2001). *Soul purpose: A practical guide for creating a life you love.* Campbellville, ON: Life on Purpose Publishing.

Ball, P.J. (2001). *A woman's way to wisdom: Through an understanding of her sexuality & relationships.* London, UK: Arcturus Publishing Ltd.

Behrendt, G. & Tuccillo, E. (2004). *He's just not that into you: The no excuses truth to understanding guys.* New York, NY: Simon & Schuster.

Bolen, J.S. (1985). *Goddesses in every woman: A new psychology of women.* San Francisco, CA: Harper Colophon Books.

Breathnach, S.B. (1998). *Something more: Excavating your authentic self.* New York, NY: Warner Books.

Carlson, R. & Schield, B. (1990). *For the love of God: New writings by spiritual and psychological leaders.* San Rafael, CA: New World Library.

Chopra, D. (1993). *Ageless body, timeless mind.* New York, NY: Harmony Books.

Coombs, A. (2001). *The living workplace: Soul, spirit & success in the 21st century.* Toronto, ON: Harper Business.

Deida, D. (2000). *Dear lover: A woman's guide to enjoying love's deepest bliss.* Austin, TX: Plexus.

———. (1995). *Intimate communion: Awakening your sexual essence.* Deerfield Beach, FL: Health Communications, Inc.

Dyer, W.W. (2004). *The power of intention: Learning to co-create your world your way.* Carlsbad, CA: Hay House, Inc.

Emoto, M. (2004). *The hidden messages in water.* Hillsboro, OR: Beyond Words Publishing, Inc.

Esquivel, L. (1992). *Like water for chocolate: A novel in monthly installments with recipes, romances, and home remedies.* New York, NY: Doubleday.

Ford, D. (1998). *The dark side of the light chasers: Reclaiming your power, creativity, brilliance, and dreams.* New York, NY: Riverhead Books.

Foundation for Inner Peace (1996). *A course in miracles.* New York, NY: Viking.

Gawain, S. (1986). *Living in the light: A guide to personal and planetary transformation.* San Rafael, CA: Whatever Publishing, Inc.

Germer, F. (2001). *Hard won wisdom: More than 50 extraordinary women mentor you to find self-awareness, perspective, and balance.* New York, NY: Perigee.

Gladwell, M. (2000). *The tipping point: How little things can make a big difference.* New York, NY: Little, Brown & Company.

Golden, A. (1997). *Memoirs of a geisha.* New York, NY: Vintage.

Hubbard, B.M. (1998). *Conscious evolution: Awakening the power of our social potential.* Novato, CA: New World Library.

Kerner, I. (2005). *Be honest: You're just not that into him either: Raise your standards and reach for the love you deserve.* New York, NY: ReganBooks/HarperCollins Publishers.

Myss, C. (1997). *Why people don't heal and how they can.* New York, NY: Harmony Books.

Needleman, J. (1998). *Time and soul: Where has all the meaningful time gone? ... and how to get it back.* New York, NY: Currency/Doubleday.

Padus, E. (1986). *The complete guide to your emotions & your health: New dimensions in mind/body healing.* Emmaus, PN: Rodale Press.

Pert, C. (1997). *Molecules of emotion: Why you feel the way you feel.* New York, NY: Scribner.

Tolle, E. (1997). *The power of now: A guide to spiritual enlightenment.* Vancouver, BC: Namaste Publishing Inc.

Weinstein, M. (2005). *The surprising power of family meals: How eating together makes us smarter, stronger, healthier and happier.* Hanover, NH: Steerforth Press.

Williamson, M. (1999). *Enchanted love: The mystical power of intimate relationships.* New York, NY: Simon & Schuster.

Yogananda, P. (1997). *Journey to self-realization: Discovering the gifts of the soul.* Los Angeles, CA: Self-Realization Fellowship.

Recommended Reading

Anand, M. (1989). *The art of sexual ecstasy: The path of sacred sexuality for western lovers*. New York, NY: Jeremy P. Tarcher/Putnam.

Barker, R.C. (1988). *The power of decision*. Marina del Rey, CA: DeVorss & Company.

————. (1991). *Treat yourself to life*. New York, NY: Perigee.

Canfield, J. & Hansen. M.V. (1995). *The aladdin factor: How to ask for and get anything you want*. (Abridged) Audio Cassette: Audio Renaissance.

Chopra, D. (2004). *The book of secrets: Unlocking the hidden dimensions of your life*. New York, NY: Harmony Books.

Chopra, D. & Simon, D. (2004). *The seven spiritual laws of yoga: a practical guide healing body, mind, and spirit*. Hoboken, NJ: John Wiley & Sons.

Collier, R. (1966). *The amazing secrets of the masters of the far east*. Tarrytown, NY: Robert Collier Publications.

Coloroso, B. (2001). *Kids are worth it: Giving your child the gift of inner discipline*. Toronto, ON: Penguin Canada.

Deida, D. (1997). *It's a guy thing: An owner's manual for women*. Deerfield Beach, FL: Health Communications Inc.

Eyre, L. & R. (1984). *Teaching your children joy*. New York, NY: Fireside.

Fox, M. (1995). *The reinvention of work: A new vision of livelihood for our time*. New York, NY: Harper San Francisco.

Gawain, S. (1982). *Creative visualization*. New York, NY: Bantam New Age Book.

Hall, M.P. (1972). *Healing: The divine art*. Los Angeles, CA: The Philosophical Research Society, Inc.

Hay. L.L. (1984). *You can heal your life*. Santa Monica, CA: Hay House.

Hewitt, F. & Hewitt, L. (2003). *The power of focus for women: How to live the life you really want*. Deerfield Beach, FL: Health Communications Inc.

Howard, J. (2004). *A woman's journey is her legacy*. Beaverton, OR: Nita Lina.

Hillman, J. (1996). *The soul's code: In search of character and calling*. New York, NY: Time Warner Company.

Kelly, M.O. (2002). *Path of the pearl: Discover your treasures within.* Hillsboro, OR: Beyond Words Publishing.

Kingma, D.R. (1998). *A lifetime of love: How to bring more depth, meaning and intimacy into your relationship.* Berkeley, CA: Conari Press.

Muir, C. & C. (1989). *Tantra: The art of conscious loving.* San Francisco, CA: Mercury House.

Murphy, J. (1980). *The amazing laws of cosmic mind power.* West Nyack, NY: Parker Publishing, Inc.

Orman, S. (1999). *The courage to be rich: Creating a life of material and spiritual abundance.* New York, NY: Riverhead Books.

Roddick, A. (1991). *Body and soul.* London, UK: Vermilion.

Robbins, A. (1991). *Awaken the giant within: How to take immediate control of your mental, emotional, physical & financial destiny.* New York, NY: Summit Books.

Sharma, R.S. (1998). *Leadership wisdom from the monk who sold his Ferrari: The 8 rituals of visionary leaders.* Toronto, ON: Harper Collins.

Tart, C. (1987). *Waking up: Overcoming the obstacles to human potential.* Boston, MA: New Science Library.

Thoele, S.P. (1996). *Heart centered marriage: Fulfilling our natural desire for sacred partnership.* Berkeley, CA: Conari Press.

Vanzant, I. (1998). *In the meantime: Finding yourself and the love you want.* New York, NY: Fireside.

Waitley, Dr. D. (1985). *The double win: For anyone who has the desire to excel.* Old Tappan, NJ: Berkeley Books.

Walsch, N.D. (1995). *Conversations with God: An uncommon dialogue.* Charlottesville, VA: Hampton Roads Publishing.

Williamson, M. (2002). *Everyday Grace: Having hope, finding forgiveness, and making miracles.* New York, NY: Riverhead Books.

———. (1993). *A return to love: Reflections on the principles of a course in miracles.* New York, NY: Harper Collins.

Wolf, N. (1991). *The beauty myth.* Toronto, ON: Vintage.

About the Author

JENICA ASHLIE IS A SEEKER OF TRUTH. A sought-after inspirational speaker, writer and educator in the field of conscious relationships, she has met and worked with some of the 21st century's greatest thinkers. A frequent media guest and keynote speaker, she conducts workshops, retreats and training programs throughout the country. A relationship educator, she helps people experience deep intimacy and connection within their lives. As an incurable romantic and former professional matchmaker, Ms. Ashlie counsels all age groups on the intricacies of finding love and companionship.

In her work and through her presentations, seminars, retreats and training programs, Jenica's mission is to train minds to start with heart. Through this work, she seeks to foster a world of deeper love and respect between men and women both in the home and in the workplace — a process she believes will ultimately alter the destiny of our world.

With a formal educational background in psychology, public relations and the healing arts, at an earlier point in her career Jenica was hired by a multinational accounting firm to provide outplacement counseling, career coaching, and work transition support services. This experience confirmed the deep dissatisfaction felt by many professionally employed women, who frequently reported on the need they felt to sublimate their essential feminine essence to make it in the corporate world. This book is intended to address that need.

Jenica Ashlie has written 15 spiritual travelogues and memoirs over the last 30 years and is the founder of *Heartfelt Press*, a division of *Heart to Heart Communications Inc.* Ms. Ashlie lives in Calgary, Canada with her son Parker, but her gypsy heart finds respite in various places around the globe. Her vision of a world where children are witnesss to a deep love and respect between the sexes creates the possibility for peace on our planet.

An Invitation to Respond

THIS BOOK HAS BEEN AN ENDEAVOR OF LOVE, and it gives me great joy knowing that it has helped many people become all they can be.

Try the ideas you've learned from reading this book, and let me know what's worked for you.

I invite you to visit to my website, <**www.yourfeminine heart.com**>, and let me know how your life as been affected by reading this book. If you do, my next book might be co-authored by you and hundreds of other Feminine Hearts.

You and I, working together with others, will create a new era of love, one heart at a time.

Shine brightly, live life to the fullest and keep your Feminine Heart open.

In deep gratitude,

Jenica

Start with Heart – Live Inside Out™

HEART TO HEART COMMUNICATIONS INC.
Keynote Speeches, Workshops, Seminars & Consulting Services

Let JENICA ASHLIE teach you how to express your authentic self ...
increasing the well-being of individuals, families and organizations.
We create the world we all share.

*Heart to Heart Communications Inc. is an educational company
whose mission is to promote conscious relationships through
transformative experiences on an individual basis
changing the way we live, work and love.*

Since 1982, Jenica has worked with people of all ages and diversity of backgrounds,
teaching them to identify their inner passion — and how to *live inside out.*

Find out when Jenica will be in your area by visiting:
www.jenicaashlie.com

"Giving and receiving love are among life's most important activities, and the
simple act of sharing love makes the greatest positive difference in our lives.
    I would like to teach you the fundamentals of finding love who ever you are
and where ever you live."
    —JENICA ASHLIE, **author,** *Your Feminine Heart: A New Era of Love*

Now you can experience JENICA ASHLIE live during her seminar and book signing tours
across North America.

At these events Jenica will share the timeless secrets of creating a life where love is
present in all ways.

JENICA ASHLIE's message is clear: "Start with heart — live inside out. You are either
healing yourself and those around you, or adding to the demise of the planet."

Start with Heart — Live Inside Out™

E-COMMUNITY, BOOK ORDERS & CONTACT INFORMATION

I appreciate your purchase of my latest book. If you wish to order additional copies of *Your Feminine Heart*, please contact us below.

I invite you to consider joining Your Feminine Heart's community at <www.yourfeminineheart.com/book> where you may share your heart's journey with thousands of others from around the world. Embracing the gifts of your own Feminine Heart will enable you to better express your authentic self and contribute more fully to the betterment of the planet. It's an important step in becoming a co-creator of love and light — and your participation will help to bring peace to every corner of the world.

At the same website, access and enjoy our free, monthly e-zine/newsletter — full of great reminders of what can so easily be overlooked or forgotten.

Jenica ♡

Your Feminine Heart: A New Era of Love
is published and distributed in Canada by *Heartfelt Press Inc.*

IN CANADA
PO Box 86011, 2106 — 33rd Avenue SW
Calgary, Alberta T2T 6B7, Canada

IN THE UNITED STATES
c/o ELK U.S.A.
9950 South, 300 West
Sandy, Utah 84070 USA

For more information about products and services, call:
1 (866) 403 • LOVE (5683) toll free in North America

www.yourfeminineheart.com

Heartfelt Press Inc. is a wholly owned division of Heart to Heart Communications Inc.